Jill Blashack Strahan

founder of Tastefully Simple®

simply

Shine

STORIES THAT STIRRED THE FIRE

Simply Shine
Stories That Stirred the Fire
By Jill Blashack Strahan

Copyeditor: Christine Frank, www.ChristineFrank.com
Editor: Kim Pearson, www.primary-sources.com
Cover and Interior design: Toolbox Creative, www.ToolboxCreative.com

Library of Congress Control Number: 2007932680
Jill Blashack Strahan
Simply Shine: Stories That Stirred the Fire
ISBN: 978-0-9798098-0-4

Dedication

To my son, Zachary Michael.
Your spirit simply shines and makes the world smile.
I love you to the moon.

Contents

chapter five *Burning Bright*

chapter six *Choose to Shine*

chapter one

Inner Sparks

Inner Sparks

*"If I was offered for life to be perfect,
it would be tempting, but I would decline …
for life would no longer teach me anything."*

⌒— AUTHOR UNKNOWN

Life *isn't* always perfect.

It was 6:30 A.M. on August 10, 1985. Steve and I had been married only eight days, and were staying at Mom's house overnight. Mom came into our bedroom to wake us, saying in an eerily calm voice that the sheriff had just called. There was a fire at the home farm, the house that had been in our family for three generations and the home in which I'd been raised.

My brother Mike was living there.

In a stupor, we drove to the farm. As we came up the driveway we saw flames engulfing the house. There was nothing we could do except watch. Within two hours the sheriff walked solemnly across the yard to tell us that they had found my brother just three feet from the front door of the house.

I fell to my knees. He was twenty-eight years old. Twenty-eight. And just like that, my big brother was gone. No more hugs, no more dancing together, no more "Hey, Sis!" as he walked in the door with a big smile.

I was devastated. I was twenty-six years old and, as the finality of Mike's death sunk in, I was suddenly and profoundly aware of my mortality. His death made two things painfully clear to me. Life isn't perfect and our lives are short.

At the time I wasn't thankful for this searing insight. Mike's death was a tragedy and the fact that life was imperfect and *short* was a curse. His death was a meaningless waste that didn't make sense. For a long time I searched for reasons and found none. I was angry.

But over the years life has taught me this: Mike's death was one of my greatest gifts. His life enriched mine beyond measure. It became a turning point in my life, a catalyst for me to seize the day and live life fully *now*. Mike gave me a reason to go for my dreams.

In the following pages I share a collection of lessons I've learned along the way. But this is not a standard memoir. These short stories are simply based on my experiences, are not necessarily chronological, and not always flattering. But I hope they will give you what they gave me: the courage to live life more fully, with more meaning and intent. I hope that your fire will be stirred and you'll feel the flame of determination to go for your dreams.

Life *isn't* always perfect, but it is overflowing with teachings.

Priceless Experience

"Every experience is a good experience:
  it may not be a pleasant one, but every experience is a good one."

— Jill Blashack Strahan

One of my dreams was to have my own business. Today I'm blessed to say that dream came true. It's called Tastefully Simple. We're a privately owned direct-sales company headquartered in Alexandria, Minnesota. We sell easy-to-prepare gourmet food, primarily through home taste-testing parties.

Tastefully Simple was founded in 1995 on a dream and a shoestring. I was the only employee and the only salesperson, also known as a consultant. As of 2006, our annual retail sales were $120 million, we had over 300 employees at headquarters, and there were nearly 22,000 independent consultants nationwide.

Has it been easy? Absolutely not.

Has it been luck? Maybe.

Has it involved a lot of hard work? Unequivocally yes.

And by the grace of God, it has all resulted in great success, which has produced some recognition. And trust me, recognition is nice. It's fun being the Founder & CEO when business is going well. But the recognition needs to go to so many other people: those who've taught me to work smarter, and those who've learned along with me. There were a lot of them.

People will sometimes ask about the "secret" to our success. I don't have any secrets. As Susan Scott says, "Life is curly. Don't try to straighten it out." My life hasn't been a straight line. It's been very curly. Damn curly. As a matter of fact, it's been pretty *snarly* at times. I've made mistakes. I've been discouraged. I've wanted to give up. Sometimes I was overcome with inertia or was just plain tired. Sometimes I was confused. (Now that I think about it, I'm *often* confused.) I've ranted and raved like a madwoman. And at times I've been a "girl" and cried.

I also overcame adversities. I've bubbled with enthusiasm. I've been enlightened at times. I've had moments of self-described brilliance and creativity, albeit *moments*. I've experienced much joy and I've laughed until my cheeks hurt. I've been overcome by gratitude for blessings I felt unworthy of yet received just the same.

Nope. I don't have any secrets. What I have had is an exciting and eventful journey, and one that I'm still on.

I'm evolving, which is just a fancy way of saying that I'm still learning. Some of what I've learned has been great fun. Some of what I've learned has caused me deep anguish.

Regardless, all of what I've learned has been a priceless experience.

We Don't Do It Alone

"If I want to do something good, I can do it on my own.
If I want to do something GREAT, I'm going to have to develop a team."

— Dr. John C. Maxwell

In June 2000 I received the Ernst & Young Entrepreneur of the Year Award for Minnesota, North Dakota and South Dakota. I was extremely shocked and honored to have won. It was even more significant because my parents were there to witness it. After all they'd endured in their lives, it was important to me that they felt proud. They deserved it.

When I went on the Academy Awards-like stage to articulate my words of acceptance and thanks, I was unprepared. I truly was not expecting to win and was overcome with humility and gratitude. And suddenly I understood why all acceptance speeches sound the same. How can you *begin* to thank all of those who contributed? No one ever does it alone.

I thanked the good Lord, and my mom and dad, and my dear friends, and the Alexandria community, and Tastefully Simple's founding partner, Joani Nielson, and the Tastefully Simple team. I didn't have a time limit on my speech, so I regret that I didn't say more.

Because I'm *not* the one representing Tastefully Simple at every home taste-testing party held by our consultants across the nation. I'm *not* the smiling face representing Tastefully Simple as our Ambassador of First Impressions in our headquarters' lobby. I'm *not* the one representing Tastefully Simple through the excellent picking, packing and shipping of our products. I'm *not* the one representing Tastefully Simple in our contract negotiations or in the quality of our facility or mailings. I'm *not* the one representing Tastefully Simple in the prompt attention to our accounts payable or in the high-pressure inventory management function. I'm *not* the one representing Tastefully Simple in our Sales Team by addressing our consultants' day-to-day issues and challenges. I'm *not* the one representing Tastefully Simple in Team Relations when they're hiring or dealing with sensitive issues. I'm *not* the one representing Tastefully Simple during intense special projects or impromptu, immediate marketing and public relations needs. I'm *not* the one representing Tastefully Simple through superb training, graphic design and communication pieces and product development.

Bottom line: The Ernst & Young award, and any recognition we've received, truly does not belong to me. It belongs to all of the people who are ambassadors for Tastefully Simple every day. Teamwork is the bedrock of great things happening. It was in the beginning, and it still is today.

I didn't build this company. An amazing team of dedicated, passionate and loyal *people* did. As Founder & CEO, I'm deeply honored to be the spokesperson for *all* of the people who have made Tastefully Simple the success it is.

We don't do it alone.

A Dairyman's Daughter

"The best day of your life is the one on which you decide your life is your own.
 No apologies or excuses.
 No one to lean on, rely on or blame.
 The gift of life is yours;
 it is an amazing journey, and you alone are responsible for the quality of it."

— Bob Moawad

I grew up on a dairy farm near Villard, Minnesota, population 300. There were eighteen people in my high school graduating class. Villard is 20 miles away from Alexandria, a small town of approximately 20,000 people, which is 130 miles northwest of Minneapolis.

I'm one of four children, and the only girl. I never questioned that I would get married someday, probably to a farmer. Apart from that, I had no idea what I wanted.

I went off to college in the fall of 1976, attending the University of Minnesota, Morris. I planned to major in English because I didn't know what else to major in. My time at the U of M wasn't exactly a conspicuous success, to put it kindly. So I transferred to the Alexandria Technical College, enrolling in the sales program, and hoping that inspiration would strike me there.

It did. One of my class assignments was to create a plan for an imaginary business. I created a gift shop that I called Rainbow's End. Upon the encouragement of my instructor, I entered my business plan in the Minnesota DECA (Distributive Education Clubs of America) competition. To my surprise I placed second at state level and progressed to the national competition, where I was a finalist.

After graduating from Alexandria Technical College, I took a job with the local JC Penney doing displays and advertising. From there I worked in a gift shop, The Marquee Too.

Taking this job was an intentional move. Due to my Rainbow's End experience, I knew that someday I wanted to own my own gift shop. I then went on to co-own a small café, where I had a crash course in leadership and business management. After that I co-created and managed a tanning studio. Later I worked in sales at First American Bank.

I got married when I was twenty-one, divorced at twenty-four, then married again at twenty-six. My second husband, Steve, and I married in 1985, and our son, Zach, was born in 1992. Eventually I started another business, Care with Flair Gifts & Gift Baskets.

Care with Flair was a little inky-dinky business that started with selling Valentine gift baskets to people I knew. Eventually, I rented a kiosk in the Alexandria Viking Plaza mall during the Christmas and Easter seasons. As the business grew, ever so slowly, I moved into a tiny back apartment of our rental house on Tenth and Broadway in Alexandria. As it continued to grow, we moved Care with Flair into the front part of the house and *we* moved into the little efficiency apartment in the back.

Two months after we moved into the back apartment I got pregnant. When our son, Zach, was born we bathed him in the kitchen sink. And the living room was so small that I used to joke that I could vacuum the whole living room while sitting on the couch. Small is sometimes better!

Having children often has an interesting effect on new parents. Suddenly I found myself examining my life and asking if I liked what I saw. I didn't. I wasn't getting a good return on my investment of time and energy. I was spending a lot of time running Care with Flair; the shop was open six days a week, and during the Christmas season it was open every day. It was exhausting. I remember falling asleep during one Christmas Eve church service after having worked many continuous 14-hour days.

So in June 1993 I liquidated the retail store and continued selling directly to the 3,000 clients on my mailing list as well as working more with business accounts.

As you can see, there's nothing extraordinary. Just life experiences for a dairyman's daughter. But all of it, and more of the same, led me to Tastefully Simple.

Ding Ding!

"Assumption is the mother of screw-up."

— Angelo Donghia, Interior Designer

One of the things my clients often liked was the inclusion of gourmet foods in my Care with Flair gift baskets. Over the years, sales reps encouraged me to carry even more gourmet products. But I resisted.

First, I'm not a gourmet cook. As a matter of fact, I hate to cook. Well, let me rephrase. It's not that I *hate* to cook. It's just that I don't find cooking particularly therapeutic. I'd much rather work three hours later at the office than go home to cook a meal.

Second, I was skeptical that specialty food products would sell in little ol' Alexandria. I was born and raised in this area, and I knew that it was a conservative community with practical, salt-of-the-earth people. My exact thoughts were, "No one here will pay $7.95 for a jar of raspberry salsa. Gourmet food in Alexandria? I don't think so!"

Despite my reservations, I tested the concept by selling a few products. I often had open house events in my home-based shop prior to the holidays and offered taste-testings. Clients loved it, and during the Christmas open house the shop would be packed. I discovered they appreciated "experiencing" the products.

Because I no longer had a retail storefront, in the fall of 1993 I was invited to exhibit in Alexandria's annual Holiday Crafter's Tour. I was honored by the invitation; the event was very popular, had a wonderful reputation and an equally wonderful turnout. Similar to a progressive dinner, it was a progressive arts and crafts show. People would drive to five or six homes where there were approximately five artisans selling their wares in each of the homes.

It's held on the first weekend in November, during open deer hunting season. I call it "Get Back Time." The men go out and kill animals and the women jump in their car and go spend money!

I brought five gift basket themes to the Crafter's Tour, all of which included gourmet foods. I asked the organizers if I could also offer taste-testing and sell the individual products that were in the baskets. They thought it was a great idea.

The cold, windy night before the event I loaded up my blue Grand Am with cases of roughly eight products. All of them were open-and-enjoy or "low-maintenance preparation," requiring no more than two added ingredients.

I set up my displays in the kitchen, and as I finished creating a pyramid of champagne jelly jars I stepped back to survey my work. It was lovingly adorned with pine garlands, white lights and a crystal platter to hold the samples.

Suddenly I was overwhelmed by doubt. "Am I out of my *mind*?" I thought. "What on earth am I doing? There is no way anyone in Alexandria, Minnesota, is going to pay $5.95 for a tiny, four-ounce jar of champagne jelly. I'm going to have to pack up every bit of this and haul it home Saturday night."

Wrong!

The next day, there was hardly a person who didn't have one of the products in their hand as they stood in line to pay. Even though these people had not been on a quest for gourmet foods, the products were a smash hit. They were high quality, easy to prepare, ideal for entertaining and the perfect holiday gift for people who had everything. And who doesn't have someone like that on their Christmas list?

It was a two-day show, and I ran around like a mad woman, replenishing the beer bread, spinach and herb mix, creamy wild rice soup, *and* the jars of champagne jelly. By the end of the weekend, I'd sold $200 in gift baskets — and $2,500 in food!

I hollered "*Yippie skippie!*" all the way to the bank.

So now you're probably thinking to yourself, "Okay, this is the happily-ever-after part, where she tells me that this event was the catalyst to start Tastefully Simple."

Nope.

I can be a slow learner sometimes and I didn't recognize the potential until one year later when I was invited back to the Holiday Crafter's Tour to sell "Reindeer Chips."

Reindeer Chips was the flagship product of my newest business venture. I had sold my Care with Flair Gifts & Gift Baskets business in June 1994 and was now collaborating with Joani Nielson, the owner of an upscale hair salon called Salon Alexis. Together we created and manufactured Reindeer Chips, a flat pretzel chip dipped in almond bark and drizzled with red and green swirls. The Alexandria newspaper had done an article on us, which the Holiday Crafter's Tour organizers read.

My friend Glenda had again provided her home for the event, and one week before she called to tell me she needed more items at her house in order to make it look appealing and plentiful. ("You can't sell out of an empty basket," she'd quip.) She asked if, in addition to the Reindeer Chips, I could once again bring some of the gourmet food items I'd sold the previous year. I agreed and then scrambled to order some products for taste-testing.

And it happened again. By the end of two days at the Holiday Crafter's Tour, I had sold $200 in Reindeer Chips—and nearly $2,000 in food! (Yes, I "yippie skipped" my way to the bank once again.)

Two weeks later, after coming home at 3 o'clock in the morning following a late-night session of dipping Reindeer Chips with Joani, I was wide awake. Sitting in my bathroom (with the lid closed!) so I didn't disturb Zach or Steve, I flipped through *Entrepreneur* magazine. The cover of the magazine had caught my attention. It featured people who had become millionaires before the age of forty.

I came across the story of a company called Country Peddlers, now AtHome America, based in the Chicago area. Two sisters had started the company as a retail store, selling decorative household items. Then they developed a new sales channel through home parties, much like Home Interiors.

I immediately flashed back to a gift basket party that Glenda had hosted for me in 1990 when I had Care with Flair Gifts & Gift Baskets. The total party sales were over $800 and I'd been intrigued by the success. I did some minimal research on the home party concept, but having a business selling gift baskets through home parties was an entirely different animal than retailing. Plus, I was *not* a home party queen. I went to home parties on occasion but was rather indifferent to the concept. Until now. It suddenly hit me.

DING-DING!

People weren't looking for gift baskets. They were looking for exceptional, convenient food. And if people from *Alexandria, Minnesota,* were buying these gourmet food products, people anywhere in the nation would buy them. And what would be more perfect than selling these products through home taste-testing parties?

Humble Beginnings

"If at first you do succeed, try not to look astonished!"

So there I was in my bathroom at three o'clock in the morning, captivated by the idea of a home party company selling food. The more I thought about it, the more excited I became. Yes, I hate to cook. And yes, I'm not wild about home parties. But *this* would be a party I would dig attending. It would revolve around two of my favorite pastimes—talking and eating! And the food would be easy to prepare, so hating to cook was actually an advantage.

My excitement grew throughout that night and into the next day. Intuition told me that this could actually work. When I saw Joani the following morning, I shared my idea. She listened quietly while I babbled on and on. When I paused for breath she calmly yet enthusiastically said, "I would invest in that."

That was the encouragement I needed. And it wasn't about the money. It was about her belief in the idea. Joani was someone I respected. I admired her instinct, vision and business savvy, plus she had a great common-sense approach to life.

In the nights that followed, while dipping Reindeer Chips, we brainstormed how we could roll this out operationally. I did a limited amount of research on home parties, including on Creative Memories, who was headquartered 60 miles away in St. Cloud. They sold scrapbook photo albums through home classes and were willing to mentor me. And I was willing to learn.

Developing a five-year business plan was consuming and painstaking. I was continually modifying and rewriting and modifying again. Upon completion, we created an S-corp with 70 percent ownership by me and 30 percent by Joani. With Joani's $10,000 investment, my $6,000 cash injection and a $20,000 loan through Bremer Bank and the Small Business Administration, Tastefully Simple was born.

In addition to Joani's cash investment, she contributed Tastefully Simple's "headquarters": a wooden out-building with a concrete floor and no running

Inner Sparks ⌒ 23

water. Lovingly referred to as The Shed, this was located next to Joani's home on Wild West Lane in Alexandria.

To say that we "bootstrapped" is an overstatement. We were downright cheap! A rent-free building, no investment in equipment or office furniture—I packed orders on a pool table—and no employees but me. And I was an *unpaid* employee, not taking a salary for three years. I was the first and only salesperson, aka "consultant," so my income was derived solely from my commissions. The primary financial risk was the cost of my inventory and printed materials, consisting of catalogs, invitations, order forms and business cards. Now I just had to get out there and sell.

I hosted my first Tastefully Simple taste-testing party on the evening of June 15, 1995. Until April 1998, I ran Tastefully Simple during the day and conducted parties at night and on weekends.

Three months after my first party, I hired Dolly Frost to help me with bookkeeping, taking orders, packing orders and other administrative tasks. And each day for over a year, through rain or snow or dark of night, Dolly and I would run back and forth to Joani's house to use the bathroom or get water for coffee.

We moved up in the world one year later. I hired Joey Peterson and we invested in running water, complete with a bathroom. We still had some minor inconveniences, like needing to unplug the refrigerator each time we turned on the bathroom light. But we got over it.

I didn't want to spend money if I didn't absolutely have to, so we monitored our expenditures very closely. I wouldn't buy a copy machine, so we'd drive a mile into town whenever we needed to make copies. We did eventually purchase a fax machine, but I didn't want to pay for a second telephone line so we unplugged the telephone to connect the fax. Today I can safely say that we were jumping over dollars to save pennies.

I know. You're shaking your head in disbelief at my idiocy. I'm with you. I wasn't the sharpest tool in the shed! One could argue that these decisions were short-sighted business moves. On the other hand, one could also say, "What's to argue about? It worked."

Least to Most

*"Operating from least to most means
as changes are implemented in products, programs and corporations…
we are responsible for taking incremental steps…
we don't have to do it all at once."*

— CHERYL LIGHTLE
CO-FOUNDER OF CREATIVE MEMORIES

I can't begin to tell you how priceless those three words "least to most" have been for me. Least to most means you can start small, and then grow incrementally. Although the early years were stressful, there were certainly payoffs for a least to most approach. Because we started with nothing, I believe our consultants trusted us. They could relate to us because we didn't have a silver spoon in our mouths. Like them, we had to work for what we had.

Second, there's pride in building something from nothing. When we moved from The Shed to our second location on Nokomis Street in 1998, we were so excited. It was a renovated warehouse that had no bells and whistles but it felt like the Taj Mahal. Having humble beginnings helped us appreciate the simple things in life, like a loading dock, multiple phones, real desks, a bathroom light that worked, and a refrigerator that ran continuously.

It was also scary to move. It was safe being in the shed. Although we'd started paying nominal rent, we still had extremely low overhead.

I sensed Dolly's concerns one day when we were talking about possible locations. "How are you feeling about this, Dolly?" I asked.

Dolly was a great team player so I'm sure she didn't want to appear like a naysayer. Hesitantly she responded, "It's scary. Can we really afford to do this? Our expenses are so low right now."

Our new rent payment was only going to be $1,750 a month, but I understood Dolly's fear. "I understand, Dolly. But it's time we stop playing store. In order to grow Tastefully Simple we have to do this. Our goal is to exceed $1 million in sales this year and we're already out of room. Plus this is only temporary. We'll learn from being in this location and know better what we want when we move to our permanent location in a couple of years."

And we did. We were at the Nokomis Street location for a year and ten months, learning more about the business and our facility needs each day. We decided we would build a $1 million facility with 20,000 square feet of office and warehouse space. This, too, was frightening. Other than paying off a small balance on a $15,000 spontaneous loan from my mom, we were debt free.

The offset to my fear was that we were moving to the perfect location. I refused to move to an industrial park, although there were times I was nervous that we'd have no choice. My vision was very clear: I wanted to be in a location within one mile of Alexandria, in a green location with lots of trees and ideally by a lake.

Yes, I know. You're not the first person to think that I had my head in the clouds. But it's what I wanted. And we found it. It took a while and I looked at many options. In the end, Joani is the one who spotted the property, and once we drove the acreage I knew it was perfect a green location, within one mile of Alexandria, and woods and wetlands to the south. (The lake came later.)

We had eked by using the least-to-most approach with the facility. And we'd eked by with a barebones staff. But in early 1999 I finally caved in. I had to hire someone to help me. We'd achieved $1.4 million in sales in 1998 and my goal for 1999 was $3 million. And I had no management team. I needed someone at a vice-president level to devote their time to Tastefully Simple's infrastructure. Joani and I had a tax meeting in March and I told her I was going to hire a VP. I was shocked and thrilled when she said she might be interested in the position. She understood business and Tastefully Simple, she had an incredible work ethic, and I knew she could hit the floor running.

In August Joani became a part-time employee and in 2000 she sold Salon Alexis, which freed her up to become our full-time Chief Operating Officer and Vice President. She became the queen of inventory control and warehouse functions, as well as managing our construction project.

Does the least-to-most approach work? It did for us. We moved to our new facility at 1920 Turning Leaf Lane on June 17, 2000. And on time and under budget. God love Joani!

Be Abundant, Make Magic and Be Real

"Let us become the change we seek in the world."

~ MAHATMA GANDHI

From my early twenties I believed that business was amputated from the "humanness" of the real world. The work environment kept people at a distance—big desks, pin-striped suits and sterile, rigid surroundings. There was talk about work-life balance. What is *that*? Is our work not part of our life? Shouldn't we be striving for *life* balance?

I've come to the firm conclusion that there's no extracting our personal life from our business life. When we're happy and fulfilled in our personal life, it flows into our work. When we're miserable and unhappy in our work, it spews into our personal life. In the same vein, the culture of any company is driven by our *personal* life, our *personal* beliefs and our *personal* values. And for me, these philosophies developed and evolved over time.

In 1997 I decided that I needed to be clear about our philosophies at Tastefully Simple. We needed to explore our beliefs and values. So that fall Dolly, Joey, Linda Roles and I, along with facilitator Theresa Moberg, created Tastefully Simple's seven core values. Our brainstorming was stimulated by asking ourselves, "What do we *not* want to be known for as a company?" This clarity was foundational. As the company grew and others joined us, there would be no confusion about our expectations.

Because we had a small sales force and a lot of one-to-one contact with them, it was easy to share our core values and what we stood for. As time went on and our consultant numbers grew, it became clear that I needed to communicate on a more consistent basis about our expectations. So in late 2001 I drilled into our seven core values and boiled them down to our three principles: the Law of Abundancy, the Law of Magic and the Law of Realness.

The Law of Abundancy

Fostering peace of mind through win-win attitudes.

The Law of Magic

Creating positive energy through celebration and excellence.

The Law of Realness

Building trust through humbleness.

These principles and the core values they embody drive every decision at Tastefully Simple and in my personal life. Without a doubt they're in my heart and soul.

But I haven't always lived by these principles. My beliefs have transformed over time. I learned as I went along, painful as it sometimes was. Sometimes my spark flickered. Even today I sometimes forget my own principles and fall victim to my ego. I'm left to re-learn my lessons. But when I follow — really follow — the laws of Abundancy, Magic and Realness, my flame catches again.

chapter two

Be Abundant

The Law of Abundancy

fostering peace of mind
through win-win attitudes.

Be Abundant

*"If we believe there's more than enough to go around,
there will be."*

⌒— JILL BLASHACK STRAHAN

In this section, Be Abundant, I'll share some of the experiences that helped me learn the vital lessons of abundance. And abundant thinking didn't come naturally for me; that was probably because I didn't even know what it was. We don't know what we don't know.

Abundance is defined as the state of having a lot of something. Abundant means plentiful, overflowing, ample, a profusion, copious, prosperous. You get the idea. *Lots* of somethings. More somethings than you know what to do with. That's abundance.

But it's the law of *abundancy*, not abundance. Now, I've been told that "abundancy" is not actually a word. You can't find it in the dictionary. The correct word is abundance. But I don't care. At Tastefully Simple we use the word abundancy anyway. We call things like this "Tastefully Simplisms." Abundance is the condition of having plenty. It's a passive state, to have a lot of something. But abundancy is active. It's abundance in action. We're full of abundance, but we practice abundancy.

When we practice the Law of Abundancy, we know there is more than enough to go around—of everything. We can always afford to be generous. Everyone can win. When we approach life in this way, we feel at peace.

And don't forget it's the *Law* of Abundancy. It's not the *hope* for abundancy. Like the law of gravity, it means abundance is a natural condition of life. Abundancy happens every day, to everyone, all the time.

The opposite of abundancy is scarcity. It's looking at a situation or circumstance through fear. Most of us have far more experience with scarcity thinking. "Get down! You're going to fall." "Be realistic. You're just dreaming."

"Don't try that. You're going to get hurt." "Don't be different. People will laugh at you." "Don't trust them. They're out to get you."

Blah, blah, blah. We think fear. We think small. And scarcity thinking is much easier to resort to because it's a force of habit. We've learned it.

Abundancy thinking takes more effort because it's not something we often observe. You've heard it before: you can choose to see the glass half-empty or you can choose to see it half-full.

I've learned: Find a bigger glass.

What abundancy is

Teamwork

Servant hearts

Generosity

Love

Openness

Giving back

Win-win

What abundancy is not

Ego

Competitiveness

Dog-eat-dog

Self-serving

Greed

Scarcity mentality

Territorialism

Win-lose

They Let Me Work and Pay Me Too

"Work: Something made greater by ourselves and in turn makes us greater."

— Maya Angelou
FROM A 1977 INTERVIEW IN *Black Scholar*

Dad was a dairy farmer and taught me to dream. Mom was a farmer's wife who later became a school teacher and taught me to strive for excellence. Both of them taught me the importance of loving what you do.

Dad loved to farm, although at heart he was an entrepreneur. He was often on the cutting edge of whatever was new and different and was never afraid to try new things. I can safely say that he was considered a bit of a rebel. Dad certainly didn't wait until his ideas were fashionable or accepted. He got involved in ethanol in the 1980s. He experimented with using enzymes in horse feeds. For years he worked with a product called Hexacore, a highly durable construction material. His mind was always reeling with ideas about how to do things better. Life was never dull when Dad was around.

While Dad was all about dreaming, Mom was all about striving for excellence and quality. She had a passion for details and beauty, from using placemats during every meal to arranging a stunning floral arrangement with zinnias and greens cut from the flower borders around the house. "Anything worth doing is worth doing well," she'd say.

In addition, Dad and Mom loved to work. I mean, they really *loved* it. Neither was particularly driven by money or the need to acquire material things. They worked because they *enjoyed* it. This appreciation for hard work didn't originate with them; it ran rampant through my entire family. My parents inherited their love of work from their parents.

Because of his work ethic, there are many who consider Grandpa August, my father's father, to be a legend in Pope County. He did everything at breakneck speed, including driving a hay baler. My brothers, as well as other strapping young men, were tested in sweltering Minnesota heat as they frantically stacked hay bales to keep up with him.

Grandpa was a successful farmer because of his hard work and street smarts. I don't believe Grandpa farmed for the money; he farmed because he loved to farm.

From Mom's side of the family, Grandma Evelyn often quipped, "They let me work and pay me too." Grandma Evelyn was *grateful* for work. To her, work was something you prized. It really was its own reward.

I feel sad when I see people making their career decisions based on financial gain. Will that *truly* bring us peace and contentment? To me, that's not win-win. It's win-lose. We lose. As Marsha Sinetar said, "Do what you love and the money will follow."

Coming from Good Stock

"It's important for children to know they came from good stock."

ᴐ— Wayne Zimmerman
SMALL-TOWN PSYCHOLOGIST

Mom was a great storyteller.

She would tell stories about our family, sharing that Great-Grandpa Niels and Great-Grandma Kristina had eleven children and struggled to make ends meet. Great-Grandpa was a hard worker and Great-Grandma was resourceful and refined. Although it was during the Depression and they had very little, she made sure she kept the piano and that there were fresh flowers in a vase. And she was determined that her children would get a good education. It was due to her efforts that none of them quit school, which farm children often did back then. And many of the children earned college degrees to boot.

Stories about Mom's family were plentiful, particularly stories about Great-Grandpa William. He had been a single parent who raised Grandpa Walt in an era when divorce was not accepted. He smoked a pipe, had a hand-carved cane and adored Mom. She felt unconditionally loved by her Grandpa William.

In addition, there were stories about Grandma Evelyn and Great-Grandma Margaret and Great-Great Grandma Gilbride. Mom would tell about their tenacity and determination. She would talk about their good health and their sense of humor. She would share how they handled adversity with strength and grace. I can't begin to count how many times I heard Mom say, "We have strong women in our family!"

Now, were there *skeletons* in our closet? Absolutely! Our family was as screwed up as any family. But the scandalous details, although Mom would touch on them, were never the point of her stories. She told the truth; she didn't diminish the negatives or whitewash them. But she didn't wallow in them. To her, the adversities, whatever they were, were important only because they displayed our family's strengths.

I've suffered from feelings of unworthiness, and yet I always had a core belief in myself. I now know it's because I grew up believing I came from good stock. Mom understood the concept of abundance and looking for win-win. She knew the negatives were there, but she also knew the positives would always outweigh them … if we *focused* on the positives.

We can never build strength on weakness; we can only build strength on strength.

The Murkiness

"If you don't know where you are going,
any road will take you there."

— Lewis Carroll

Most of my early life I felt inadequate. However confident I may have appeared on the outside (heck, I was a cheerleader and class president, wasn't I?), inside I was full of self-doubt. I had no big, lofty aspirations for my life. I thought of myself as just an average Minnesota farm girl who graduated as one of eighteen kids in my class.

I rarely dated. Because of my low self-esteem, I didn't feel comfortable interacting with boys. When someone asked me out on a date, I was a bit befuddled. Why would he be asking *me* out?

And I was very tentative about having children. Who was I to think I'd be a good mom? What did I have to offer a child?

As far as a "career" goes, I was clueless! When I graduated in 1976, I had no clear vision of what my life would look like. I was envious of my best friend, Mechelle. She knew from the time she was in grade school that she wanted to be a nurse when she grew up. But I couldn't see my future; it was a murky, nebulous nothingness. I felt defective.

My mom, on the other hand, had no such doubts about me. She saw me as confident and self-assured; a person full of ambition who would go after whatever she wanted come Hell or high water. She knew I would go to college after high school. From the time my brothers and I were little, she'd saved $10 per month so she could help us with the tuition.

Mom's positive thoughts hadn't worn off on me. I focused on my weaknesses and what I was lacking. In retrospect, what I was doing was practicing the shadow side of the Law of Abundancy. I was mired in scarcity thinking when it came to looking at my strengths.

After graduation, I went along with Mom's vision because I had no vision of my own. I went off to the University of Minnesota, Morris. In 1976, there weren't a lot of opportunities for women. And if there were, girls like me didn't know about them. I was a farm girl from a small town, and I had small thinking to match. When I thought about it, which wasn't very often, I figured I could be a teacher, a nurse or a secretary. Since I got A's in English, I loosely decided to become an English teacher. And Mom perceived me as a college graduate, so I climbed on her dream for me.

Here's what I learned: It's okay to be unclear about what we want in life. Mom's vision didn't help me see my future, but in the absence of my own vision I feel blessed that *she* had one. Although I didn't stay in college, it was a great experience. And in a weird kind of way, Mom *did* help me start to craft what I wanted out of life. She helped me learn what I didn't want—to be a college student or an English teacher.

Reap What You Sow

"You are what you choose.
One year from today, your life is going to be better or worse than it is today.
You cannot not choose."

— DR. PHIL, ON "DR. PHIL SHOW"

There's no way of getting around it. We will always reap what we sow.

Once in college, I spread my imaginary wings, reveling in new-found freedom — no one looking over my shoulder telling me when to be where, no one harping on me about getting my homework done, no one clipping those new-found wings. I often slept in. I went to class only when I deemed it necessary. I crammed at the last minute. And I jokingly say that I majored in socialization.

With just a little effort I could have had A's, but I opted for mediocrity. I was operating in a classic scarcity mode. I thought that if I took the time to study, I might be missing out on something else that was more fun. It never occurred to me that I could have fun and learn something too. I took the easier, softer way and I reaped what I sowed — which wasn't a heck of a lot!

This was brought forcibly home to me when I received my grade in English composition. I was a good writer in high school and had always received A's in English. I was humbled when I saw that my professor, the head of the English Department no less, had given me a D on one of my papers.

Although it certainly didn't feel like it at the time, that D was a great gift. Now let's keep in mind that I didn't have a passion for becoming an English teacher. I didn't know what I wanted in life and I certainly didn't have a clear sense of self. That D changed my idea of who I wanted to be, and what I wanted to do. Although it didn't convince me I was a bad writer, it did give me the push I needed to really look at my reasons for being in college.

At the end of my freshman year I knew I didn't want to study English. I didn't want to be an English teacher. And socializing was fun, but to my knowledge those skills wouldn't translate into a career. Just exactly what I wanted still wasn't clear, but at least I knew what I *didn't* want.

It was my brother Mike who suggested I enroll in the Sales Associate course at the Alexandria Technical College. He was in the program, having a great time and learning a lot too. I was intrigued with the idea, and intuitively I knew it was the right thing to do.

Mike convinced me that even if I wasn't sure about my vision for the long term, in the short term I could at least reap some benefits. So I sowed my seeds, watered and weeded them, and they grew.

Mr. Holscher Believed In Me

"A new idea is delicate.
It can be killed by a sneer or a yawn;
it can be stabbed to death by a joke
or worried to death by a frown on the right person's brow."

— CHARLES BROWER
FORMER PRESIDENT OF BBDO ADVERTISING

When I was a student at the Alexandria Technical College in the Sales Associate course, a very pivotal class was one that was devoted to creating a business plan for an imaginary business—any kind we wanted. I decided it would be cool to create an imaginary gift shop.

As a farm girl, I didn't get to town often but when we did, it was a special treat. Mom and I would go to The Marquee Too gift shop in downtown Alexandria. It wasn't really about the shopping as much as it was about the *experience.* I remember the smells of potpourri and soaps and incense. I remember the soft lighting and the music playing overhead. I remember my intrigue when I saw something unique. And I remember the beautiful displays and ambience. The Marquee Too warmed my soul.

My class project had many components, from the start-up investment, to the store lay-out, to naming the business. I named the imaginary gift shop "The Rainbow's End." It was a fun and exciting project, largely because I could see something coming to life in front of my eyes.

In addition to being graded on the business plan, each February there was a state DECA (Distributive Education Clubs of America) competition, in which technical colleges competed. Several of us from the Alexandria Technical College chose to participate in the Individual Development event, which involved presenting our business plan to a panel of judges.

I felt ill-prepared for the presentation, and after walking out the door following the judging I was relieved. I told my friends that at least I could relax at the awards ceremony that night because I had *tanked.*

I can't begin to express my shock when they announced that I'd taken second place. Lyle Holscher was my instructor. When the awards ceremony was over, Lyle informed me that I would qualify to compete at the national DECA conference in Washington, DC.

As the national conference drew closer, Lyle and I began to discuss how I could improve my presentation and how to enhance my visual aids. Between the two of us, we decided we could design a wooden board with a rainbow on it. Each color of the rainbow would signify an area of importance in a successful business, such as the marketing plan or great customer service. They would be removable, so I could unveil to the judges each of these concepts, one by one. At the end of the rainbow, there would be a pot of gold, which when removed would display my profit.

Now, I just wasn't sure how to execute the idea. Mr. Holscher came to my rescue and offered to help. The end result was a three-by-five-foot plywood presentation board, stained a dark walnut color, with each rainbow color hand painted. It was pretty awesome. (Awesome but *heavy*!)

Mr. Holscher did the woodworking all by himself, at home, at night. When I think back on his commitment and dedication, I'm overwhelmed with gratitude. How many teachers would take the time to do this for one of their students? He spent his own time, money and energy to create something for a nineteen-year-old girl who came late to class, who often complained because we were required to attend class, and who was many times a bit out of control and unruly.

Mr. Holscher was a kind, giving person. He gave selflessly and didn't look for financial gain. He gave for the sake of giving. And he showed me that he *believed* in me. He didn't express his belief in mere words. He showed me through his actions.

What Every Woman Manager Needs

"Believe it and you'll see it."

— DEWITT JONES

My first "real" job after completing the Sales Associate course at the
Alexandria Technical College was interning at the local JC Penney doing
displays and advertising. It wasn't a gift shop, but it was the retail world and
it taught me a lot.

I received the job offer while I was on vacation in California with my brother
Mike. I'd interviewed before I left and the manager, Janet Mork (Thorkelson),
tracked me down at my Uncle Wally's home to ask if I'd like the job.

"I'm honored, Mrs. Mork, but I have to be honest. Most of the time I
skipped out of my display class because I was preparing for the state DECA
competition. I'm not sure I'm qualified to do displays and advertising for you."

"Well, you came highly recommended by Lyle Holscher. I'm willing to take
the chance if you are," she said.

I hesitantly agreed. And it was a great learning experience, although often
very humbling. JC Penney was moving from their downtown location to a new
store in the Viking Plaza Mall. When the district manager came to help "blitz"
the store, he did the initial displays—thank *God*! He talked about doing a
header display, and when I gave him a dazed and confused look, I could tell
that he knew Mrs. Mork was in trouble.

But I learned as I went along and when I'd worked at JC Penney for a little
over a year, I was offered a position at The Marquee Too, the same downtown
gift shop I had loved as a teenager. I'd earn about $3.50 an hour so the pay was
less, and they offered no benefits. But I knew in my heart it was the right thing
to do. It would be great exposure to the gift industry and JC Penney couldn't
offer that.

I liked my job at Penney's. Mrs. Mork was a savvy, gentle woman whom I
considered a pioneer. It was 1978 and she was one of very few women managers

within the company. I didn't realize it at the time, but she was a mentor and role model to me.

Faced with the prospect of hiring and training a new employee, Janet could have been upset when I told her I was quitting. She could have pressured me and questioned my rationale in taking a lower-paying job with no benefits. Instead she practiced the Law of Abundancy, and on my last day of work she presented me with a going away card. Inside the card was a brass key chain shaped like a big, huge safety pin. Her handwritten note read, "What every woman manager needs."

Janet planted a seed for me. I'd never envisioned myself as a "manager" before. With those five words, she drew a mental image of who I could be. She was saying, "I believe in you." She had modeled her leadership and now she was passing the baton to me. There are few things in life that are more powerful.

Accept, Don't Expect

"A true friend knows your weaknesses but shows you your strengths;
feels your fears but fortifies your faith,
sees your anxieties but frees your spirit,
recognizes your disabilities but emphasizes your possibilities."

— WILLIAM ARTHUR WARD

It was 6:00 in the evening on the day after Thanksgiving and I was beginning to panic.

I had owned Care with Flair Gifts & Gift Baskets for a couple of years and had recently opened my twelve-by-fifteen-foot shop, "cleverly hidden on Tenth and Broadway." I was grateful to be nestled into the warmth of my little shop on this cold winter's night, and at the same time I was in an emotional and mental downward spiral.

The day after Thanksgiving was supposed to be the largest retail day of the year and frankly, my sales were ranking very high on the Suck-O-Meter. I had started the morning with grandiose visions of clients streaming in, scurrying around with armloads of gifts for their loved ones, and eventually forming an eager line to my cash box. (I couldn't afford a cash register.) Ahhhh ... the hustle and bustle of the holidays! I'd been so excited about the possibilities.

But here it was 6:00 in the evening of the biggest retail selling day of the year, and I hadn't had a single sale. (Well, *Mom* had made a $150 purchase, but that doesn't count.)

Just as I was focusing very diligently on my panic, the door opened and in breezed Cousin Roxy. Roxy is an artist and has a wonderful flair for drama. A love child of the Sixties, she lives on a hundred-year-old farm, fires porcelain wares, is a vegan and drinks green tea. She often wears Russian hats and, on this particular evening, was wearing a purple tie-dyed dress complemented by purple hair. Most importantly, Roxy is one of the wisest people I know.

We exchanged long hugs and she sat down by my desk (adorned with the empty cash box). Roxy doesn't beat around the bush with superficial conversations. She always gets down to real things that matter. And it didn't take me long to get real.

"Geez, Roxy. This is scary. Today is supposed to be the best retail day of the year. If that's true, I am in *big* trouble."

She listened while I babbled on and on about my woes and the dangers of not having the sales I needed and the fact that my business was probably going down the tubes. She never said a word. She just sat there listening with this calm, constant gaze. When I finally finished my venting, Roxy looked me straight in the eye and, with a slight tilt to her head and a gentle smile, said, "Accept, don't expect!"

We sat in silence for what seemed like an eternity as I tried to absorb her wisdom. With Roxy's one simple phrase, I realized that I was placing expectations on myself. I was wrapped up in a mentality of control and scarcity. I wasn't seeing the abundance and possibilities anymore. I wasn't having faith.

It's taken me time to realize that peace and happiness and "success" come from *trusting*. It comes from trusting that, if we've done everything we can do, whatever happens in our lives is exactly as it's meant to be. We don't have to think it to death. Sometimes we simply have to let go, accept and know that it's happening for a reason and that it's for our ultimate good.

Accept, don't expect.

You Can't Fall Off the Bottom

"Take risks.
You can't fall off the bottom."

BARBARA PROCTOR
ADVERTISING EXECUTIVE

I admit it. I was stuck. My wheels were spinning and I needed help to move forward.

In June 1993, I had liquidated my retail store, Care with Flair Gifts & Gift Baskets, and kept only my mailing list of 3,000 clients. For a year, I sold my gift baskets through direct mailings, open house events and presentations to potential business accounts. Following the busy holiday season, I became restless. I'm an all-or-nothing kind of woman and I had one foot in Care with Flair and one foot out. I felt like I was in Purgatory.

It was February 1994 and I was in my home office paying business bills that I kept in my old, frayed manila Accounts Payable folder. A one-page promotional flier from the Zig Ziglar Corporation caught my eye. It was an "Over the Top" flier that I'd kept for over two years.

When I'd received the information I'd been intrigued but had not pursued it. We had no money, so I didn't take the time to call to see what the program entailed. I'd assumed it was a Zig Ziglar weekend motivational "pep fest" in Dallas, Texas. Don't get me wrong. I was a cheerleader in high school and I'm the first to understand the value of an inspiring rah-rah pep fest. My challenge was that I knew it would be a large investment in the registration fee as well as the travel costs. Quite simply, I couldn't afford it. So I filed the information in my A/P folder with the dream of someday being able to afford it.

On this particular February morning, I pulled out the flier and read it thoroughly, lingering on the toll-free telephone number at the bottom of the page. And then I began to argue with myself.

Scarcity Voice: "Jill, don't call. You know you can't afford it."

Abundancy Voice: "Don't be ridiculous, Jill. What's the worst thing that can happen if you call?"

Scarcity Voice: "But Jill, you have no money so you're just going to be frustrated when you can't go to Dallas."

Abundancy Voice: "Come on, Jill. Call them. Nothing ventured, nothing gained. What do you have to lose if you just call and *ask*? At least you'll know what you're saying 'no' to."

This time the Abundancy Voice prevailed. I called the toll-free number.

I learned that I was half right about "Over the Top." I was wrong about it being a motivational pep fest; it was a twelve-week mentoring and coaching program via telephone that promised to help me focus on my personal goals.

I was right about it being expensive. The cost was $1,295.

That was a challenge. Steve and I lived very modestly. Hand-to-mouth is a more accurate description. We had next to nothing in our savings account, eked out our house payment each month, and juggled our bills to drag payments into the following month whenever possible. $1,295 was a ton of money. And I was adamantly opposed to putting this expense on our credit card.

In spite of this, Steve encouraged me to do it. After an emotional tug of war, I did it. I needed to figure out what I wanted in my life. I called them back, bit the bullet, and put the fee on our credit card. I considered it an investment rather than an expense.

And heck, you can't fall off the bottom!

Everything Happens for a Reason

"That is the power of having a goal,
writing it down, believing it will happen,
and knowing that, if it is for your ultimate good, it will happen."

~ MIKE HAYNIE

Mike Haynie was my Over the Top coach. He called me weekly to discuss the goals I'd defined a week earlier. The focus of my goals was on Zig Ziglar's seven categories:

Spiritual   Physical

Family   Financial

Career   Mental

Social

In addition, I listened to Zig Ziglar cassette tapes, read See You at the Top, and completed the companion workbook. It was an intense twelve weeks and a big investment of my time and energy.

One area in which I struggled was in setting family goals. I suspect that my struggle stemmed from my family experience as a farm girl. We worked. It's what we did best. Like many farm families, our personal value was defined by how much we accomplished in a day. Taking a vacation was simply not done.

Zach was nearly two years old when I was working with Mike, and I knew I wanted him to have a strong work ethic. I also knew that I wanted him to learn how to have balance in his life and how to have fun. I wanted him to have family memories that were carefree and that weren't only work oriented.

So after considerable deliberation, I finally landed on a family goal. It was a huge leap for me. I wanted to have a one-week vacation with Steve and Zach. This "ideal vacation" would be at a resort, but nothing fancy. Just a sleepy little resort with a cabin on a lake. You know the kind. Where you can simply *be*: swimming, reading by the fire, relaxing on the deck.

Well at least I'd accomplished defining the goal. But there was a pretty big snag. Once again, even though it was a relatively low-budget vacation, it seemed financially impossible. It required money, something we did *not* have.

I shared my skepticism with Mike. He told me not to worry about that right now. Just focus on the steps necessary to make it happen.

I blindly followed his advice. I researched Minnesota resorts that met my lakeside criteria and I found the perfect spot. I called them for more information. A two-bedroom cabin was $700 a week, but it had its own kitchen so we could save money by cooking all of our meals.

I reserved it for a one-week stay. As they asked for my credit card number to secure the reservation, I felt a knot in my stomach. How I was going to pay for this? I had only three months to figure it out because I did not want this debt on our credit card.

Regardless of the knot in my stomach, booking that one-week stay at Vacationaire Resort was a huge victory for me. It required faith. I knew in my heart that the vacation was right for all of us. It was a small part of what I thought our ideal life could be—for Steve, for Zach and for me.

Nonetheless, it was frightening. But to be true to myself and my family, I knew I needed to ignore those fears.

I should add, although it's a bit embarrassing, that I had devised a *very* itemized and bare-bones budget. I determined that the entire vacation would cost us $1,200, including gas, groceries, renting a pontoon for three hours, having dinner in the lodge one night, and renting a high chair for Zach. (I *said* it was very itemized!)

Twelve hundred dollars! That was a lot of money. When Mike called me for our weekly phone session, I once again expressed my apprehension. I shared my reluctance to go into debt for something so "non-essential."

Mike didn't waste many words. He simply asked me to trust.

The following week, my Aunt Toots (Note: only *family* can call her Toots) drove up the driveway. As we were visiting, she pushed an envelope across the dining room table. She said that my Grandpa August, who was then in his nineties, had decided to give $10,000 to each of his grandchildren.

I was utterly speechless. To this day, when I think back on that moment, I feel breathless. It was a miracle.

When I next spoke to Mike I was still incredulous. "You are not going to believe this. I have the money for our vacation!"

And Mike said something I've never forgotten. He said, "That is the power of having a goal, writing it down, believing it will happen, and knowing that, *if it is for your ultimate good*, it will happen."

It was a defining moment in my life, truly a spiritual awakening. I sat there mesmerized, with the phone in my hand, absorbing the significance of what he had just shared with me: " … and knowing that, if it is for your ultimate good, it will happen."

That was the missing link for me. *That* was why I had resisted setting goals in the past. I had believed that if I didn't achieve my goal, I would have "failed." Translation: I would be a failure.

Here was my huge Aha!: *My goals were not all about ME.* If I did everything I could to achieve my goals and if they didn't come to fruition, it was not that I was a failure. It didn't mean that I "failed." It was simply that it was not meant to be. Plain and simple. It was not meant to be. There was a bigger plan for me and I didn't need to know what that plan was.

If it is meant to be, it will be. Everything happens for a reason.

Giving With Gratitude

"Tithing is a way of showing gratitude
for whoever or whatever you feel is responsible for the gift of life.
It's paying your rent to live in this world.
It's your share of the air you breathe,
the color of the trees,
the sun in the morning and the moon at night.
It's also a most tangible way of saying,
'Thank you. I have more than I need.'"

                         — JOHN-ROGER AND PETER McWILLIAMS

During our coaching calls, Mike began to see that I had some mental and spiritual barriers about money. The most I'd ever earned was $14,000 a year and I had to stretch myself to set a five-year goal of earning $30,000.

So he gave me an assignment. I was to read twenty pages, from page 457 to 477, of the book *Wealth 101* by John-Roger and Peter McWilliams, which discussed tithing and seeding. Actually that was an excellent strategy. Had he asked me to read the entire book, I wouldn't have taken the time. (Although I did end up reading the whole book!)

Those twenty pages were compelling, and I became more and more excited. I'd first experienced the power of tithing when I was nineteen years old. I lived in an apartment above the Andria Theatre in downtown Alexandria and was working full time at The Marquee Too gift shop. I grossed $400 per month and couldn't afford to buy groceries the majority of the time. I lived on brown rice mixed with stewed tomatoes, green beans and hamburger. It was tasty, healthy *and* cheap!

One night I saw a television commercial about sponsoring a World Vision child. As I watched it, I was filled with gratitude for the life I had, and I committed to sponsoring a child for $18 per month. And miraculously, I always had enough to send that $18.

At that time I hadn't viewed it as a lifelong commitment. I'd always connected tithing to religion and the church. Nearly fifteen years later, I learned that tithing was *not* about giving to a church so they could meet their annual budget. It was giving ten percent of my income to causes greater than myself, causes I believed in. It was giving back in gratitude for what I've been given and without thought about whether or not I'd receive anything in return.

I hesitantly broached the topic of tithing with Steve. I was tentative about discussing it. What if he disagreed with me? What if I couldn't persuade him that this was the right thing to do?

But Steve agreed immediately. In mere minutes, we decided to tithe and give ten percent of our income to a cause greater than us. It could be a non-profit organization, or not. It could be the church, or not. Whatever we felt at the time was for a greater good.

I want to be very clear. This was *not* a religious decision. It was a spiritual decision. It was the sincere belief—and faith—that life was not about scarcity. A great life is about abundance and knowing there is more than enough for all of us. I learned that I'd been mentally and emotionally "attached" to money. I started internalizing the concept of "gold like dust"—if we wipe away the dust, we can be assured it will come back. If we give away our gold, we can also be assured that it will come back. I began to have faith that whatever we gave would come back to us tenfold. I knew in my heart that tithing was the right thing to do.

Now, please allow me to provide some perspective. Back in 1994, our decision to tithe was *not* going to be the shot heard around the world. Steve and I agreed that each month we would give ten percent of our income to a cause greater than us. News flash! Mathematical computation! Ten percent of nothing … is nothing! Our annual household income was probably $25,000. Obviously, we weren't going to be gifting great sums of money.

Regardless of our income, the decision was frightening because we chose to give ten percent *before* we paid any bills. We gave ten percent *before* we paid our mortgage. We gave ten percent *before* we paid for groceries. We gave ten percent *before* we bought Pampers for Zach. I experienced a physical reaction as I wrote those tithing checks. I could barely breathe.

After we'd been tithing for a couple of months, I received Grandpa's $10,000 gift. And I have no doubt that $10,000 gift of money from Grandpa

August was a blessing that resulted from tithing. To be true to my commitment, I chose to give away ten percent, which was $1,000. I was literally sick to my stomach as I wrote that anonymous check. I kept thinking about all of the things that we could do with $1,000. We could pre-pay on our mortgage, make an additional car payment, put the money in savings, or buy any of a hundred other things that we wanted.

But we tithed the $1,000. We then spent $1,200 on our vacation that I'd set as a goal; Steve *insisted* we buy a new couch and chair for $1,800; and the remaining $6,000 went into our savings account. Nearly one year later, that $6,000 was the money I used to invest in Tastefully Simple, along with Joani's $10,000.

Writing that $1,000 check led to another spiritual awakening. I realized that each time I wrote a check, it allowed me the opportunity to say a prayer of gratitude for all we had, and think of so many others who live with so much less.

Was tithing a scary commitment? Was I pushed out of my comfort zone? Absolutely. But you know what? It's not faith if you're not scared.

More Miracles

After defining my goal to have a family vacation, I realized that my ultimate goal was to have this vacation *every* year. Going to Vacationaire Resort would cost us $1,200 a year, but I was on a roll with this whole goal-setting thing!

I felt a bit greedy as I shared this with Mike. "Mike, I know I just received a huge blessing with Grandpa's gift of money. But I need to tell you that my ultimate goal is to have this vacation *every* year. I just don't know how I'm going to pay for it next year."

Mike's response? "Write it down!" (Duh! I'm slow to catch on.)

About a week later, Aunt Toots came up the driveway again. As you can imagine, I'm beginning to *really* like seeing Aunt Toots come up the driveway! As we're visiting, guess what she did. She slid an envelope across the table to me. (No, I'm *not* kidding.) And then she informed me that Grandpa August had decided to give another gift of money to all of his grandchildren over the next seven years.

Spellbound, I cautiously opened the envelope as she explained that the money would be sent to us as a quarterly distribution for seven years.

The quarterly check was for $343.

My mind was reeling. A quarterly distribution of $343. This $343 times four quarters equaled $1,372 per year. This $1,372 minus ten percent for tithing equaled $1,236 for seven years.

Our vacation budget was $1,200.

Would *you* be a believer in the power of tithing—and what goes around comes around?

Know Your Purpose

"How we spend our days is how we spend our lives."

— ANNIE DILLARD

After about six weeks and several assignments, Mike threw me a curve ball. My assignment that week was to write my life purpose. I didn't protest aloud but my thoughts were screaming. "Write my life *purpose*?! Oh, right! Just write my life purpose and define why I was put on this earth? Are you out of your *mind*?"

Obviously, I wasn't too open to the idea. The mere thought of doing it overwhelmed me. Nevertheless, I knew Mike would be calling at 10:30 next Wednesday morning to see if I'd accomplished my (*his*) goal. I followed his suggestions and over the next few days recorded things that I had done throughout my life that I really enjoyed doing, things that I felt I was good at. It was a fascinating process.

Where I had difficulty was summarizing all those experiences into a two- or three-sentence life purpose. On Tuesday morning my cousin Roxy called to ask if I wanted to come out to her house and have lunch. Procrastinator that I was, I said nothing about my plans to write my life purpose, and I accepted her invitation.

Roxy and I chatted and laughed over lunch, and then she suddenly said, "I've got to show you something," and handed me a piece of paper. "I found this in a box of old stuff," she explained. "Many years ago, when I was at Macalester College, I wrote about my dream life. I'd completely forgotten about writing it."

I looked down at the paper. Over twenty years before, Roxy had written that she wanted to live on a farm, grow her own vegetables, have a barn, raise chickens and live as close to nature as possible.

I was speechless as I read it. It was an exact description of her current life. Second, she didn't know that I should have been at home working on my assignment to write *my* life purpose.

When I got up to leave, Roxy gave me a big hug and handed me a book. "I just read this book and it's excellent. You're welcome to borrow it." She handed me *Return to Love* by Marianne Williamson.

I took the book and thanked her. To be honest, though, I was just being polite. I knew I wasn't going to take the time to actually read it. I was busy, you know. For one thing, I had this stupid assignment to write my life purpose—and it was due tomorrow morning!

When I got home I went into my office and sat down at my desk, waiting to be inspired. I just couldn't get into it. I picked up Roxy's book that was lying on my desk (conveniently located for my procrastination ease), and thumbed through it, skimming various sections. Within seconds, the book opened to the career chapter where I read this excerpt:

"Our deepest fear is not that we are inadequate.
Our deepest fear is that we are powerful beyond measure.
We ask ourselves,
'Who am I to be brilliant, gorgeous, talented, fabulous?'
Actually, who are you not to be?
You are a child of God.
Your playing small doesn't serve the world.
There's nothing enlightened about shrinking
so that other people won't feel insecure around you.
We are all meant to shine, as children do.
We were born to make manifest the glory of God that is within us.
It's not just in some of us; it's in everyone.
And as we let our own light shine,
we unconsciously give other people permission to do the same."

— MARIANNE WILLIAMSON, FROM A RETURN TO LOVE

As I sat at my desk with Marianne Williamson's book in hand, unexpected tears streamed down my face. I knew deep in my soul the truth of what she said. I realized that for most of my life I'd felt unworthy. I felt unworthy of dreaming, so I wouldn't *allow* myself to dream. I felt guilty about wanting to do more with my life. I felt uncomfortable about having high expectations. I felt arrogant if I believed I could do something well. I had been shrinking in order to please others.

The words seeped into my heart and into my core. I knew that I had a responsibility to shine, if for no other reason so that others would have permission to do the same.

My life changed at that very moment. I have no doubt that God placed Mike Haynie in my life that spring to write my life purpose. I have no doubt that God placed Roxy in my life that day to open my heart to *shining* in life.

Don't Settle

"It is a funny thing about life;
if you refuse to accept anything but the best, you very often get it."

‿— W. Somerset Maugham

With Mike Haynie's coaching, I sold Care with Flair Gifts & Gift Baskets in June 1994. It was a turning point for me. I was venturing into unknown territory. It felt like I'd stepped off a cliff. It was a confusing, frustrating, and once again murky time. I believe this is why many people don't make changes in their life. It's hard to let go of what we know and step into something we don't.

As a way to organize my thoughts and gain clarity, I decided to write down what my perfect job would be. What would get me jazzed every day? What kinds of things would I want to do that would tap into my passion? If I could have the best job in the whole wide world, what would it look like? The list of characteristics in my ideal job included:

A flexible schedule so I could be home with Zach, who was two years old.

Being creative.

Doing marketing "stuff" where I had control over a consistent "wow" image and brand.

Selling and being with people ... but not all the time.

Training and speaking publicly ... but not all the time.

Travel ... but not all the time.

And, as an afterthought, I thought, "What the heck. This is my ideal job, so I'd want an unlimited income!"

I shared this list with a few of my closest friends and, not surprisingly, some of them tilted their heads and raised their eyebrows in disbelief. "Oh *right*, Jill!" they scoffed (lovingly). "Aren't you asking a little much? You'll never find a job like that!"

I was frustrated by their response. "But why not start with what you *really* want out of life? Why not set the bar high? I can always move my bar down. But why settle for less before I even start? I would always regret that," I responded.

Three months later, on November 14, 1994, at 3 A.M., the idea for Tastefully Simple was born. The gift of my "ideal job" was presented to me and I knew by the level of my excitement that it was "right." Tastefully Simple provided me with all of the elements of my perfect job. And whether the company succeeded or failed, I knew in my heart that there would be value in the journey.

No matter how "unrealistic" other people may think our dreams are, we *can* achieve it. We don't have to settle for less. Once we take a leap of faith and define what we really want in life, once we feel it deep in our soul, then if it is for our ultimate good, we *will* attract it into our life.

I don't just believe this. I've experienced it.

Obstacles We Need

*"We often don't realize it,
but we frequently come face-to-face
with the exact obstacle we need at just the right time,
to sharpen us where we need it most."'*

⌒— TOMMY NEWBERRY

It was late summer in 1997, and I was becoming very frustrated at the snail's pace of Tastefully Simple's growth.

The first two years had reinforced for me the amazing power of goal-setting. In 1995 my goal was to have five consultants selling our products. At the end of the year, I had exceeded that goal and had a whopping seven independent consultants.

In 1996, my goal was to have thirty salespeople and by years end, we had thirty-three consultants. Once again, goal achieved.

My goal for 1997 was to have one hundred consultants, but it was August 10 and we had only thirty-one consultants. To make matters worse, I'd been meeting with potential consultants throughout the year and had not recruited *one single person.* I was incredibly discouraged.

On this particular summer day I had a meeting scheduled with another potential consultant, and at the last minute, the meeting fell through. Even though my head told me this wasn't the first time, or the last, that cancellations would happen, on the drive back to Alexandria I cracked. I bottomed out. I cried. I pounded the steering wheel. I think I may have even cursed. (Okay … I *know* I cursed.) It was an ugly sight. I was downright angry.

After an hour of driving and cursing and spewing steam, I heard a news report on Minnesota Public Radio. It was about Patty Wetterling, whose son Jacob had been abducted eight years before, when he was eleven years old. Patty was now circulating computer images around the nation of what Jacob might look like at the age of eighteen.

The angry, frustrated Scarcity Voice inside my head suddenly went silent. I was ashamed. In comparison to Patty, my problems were nothing. I said aloud,

"Now *that*, Jill, is faith and perseverance! Patty has not given up after all these long, painful years. Stop your pathetic whining and grow up. There are worse things in life!"

The next day I made a decision to stop focusing on what I *didn't* have. "I don't have enough consultants!" "I can't recruit anymore." "I don't have what it takes to make this work." "The business isn't growing anymore."

Wahhhh! It was all about what I *didn't* have.

Well, you know what? Business isn't always easy. *Life* isn't always easy. As a matter of fact, it can be doggone tough and very disappointing at times. And here's the news flash: we can't control outcomes. We can only control our response to circumstances.

So I decided to instead focus on what I *did* have. I needed to focus on solutions. Knowing I wasn't going to hit my original sales goal without having additional consultants on board for the first eight months of the year, I cut my 1997 revenue projections in half. I then adjusted the business plan for subsequent years.

And it felt good. Prior to having that emotional shift, I was wrapped up in fear. The business had flatlined and I was sucked into the sewer of decline, discouragement and negativity. I was lured into a victim mentality and subconsciously I was afraid I was failing. And when I'm afraid, I focus on scarcity, not abundancy. Once I chose to let go of my scarcity mentality and accept life on life's terms, I was at peace.

This was a big shift for me because I hadn't wanted to "give up" on my goal. Once I understood that I wasn't giving up, I redefined my goals and released myself from the past so I could look ahead at the abundance and the possibilities. The year 1997 ended with fifty-five consultants.

We can't control outcomes. We can only control our responses to life's circumstances. Life will always present us with obstacles; in truth, although we may not always welcome them, they are usually exactly what we need.

The Little Green Man

"You can't chase two rabbits and catch them both."

⌒— Author Unknown

I'm often asked if I ever got so discouraged that I was tempted to give up. Absolutely.

My income was derived from conducting Tastefully Simple parties and from the Leadership Cheques I earned based on the sales of my team. I ran the business by day and had parties at night.

After doing this for nearly three years, working an average of 70 hours per week, I knew in my heart that I was being short-sighted. It wasn't realistic to focus my attention on building my personal business *and* doing a good job on the marketing and the training and the conferences and the product line and the financials, etc, etc, etc.

First, I couldn't do it *physically*; I was exhausted.

Second, Tastefully Simple was not going to grow as a company when I had a divided focus. I couldn't chase two rabbits and catch them both. I needed to focus on the success of the company as a whole.

Third, my personal business was suffering because I wasn't having as many parties, resulting in a negative impact to my income. And that was a big problem for our financial state. Steve was self-employed too, and we needed my income to help pay our bills. Consequently we were three months delinquent in our mortgage payments. We started getting notices. First we got polite notices, then polite-yet-firm notices, then just plain "firm" notices, and finally, we received nasty notices.

One day I braced myself and called the mortgage company. I went outside so Dolly and Joey couldn't hear me, and I sat on the wooden bench outside the shed. It was a glorious spring day. But I barely noticed.

My entire attention was focused on the phone call I was having. I kept getting transferred from one person to another, having to explain my situation over and over, and receiving no straight answers. This went on for over an hour. Finally when yet another person was going to transfer me, I began to cry. "*Please* don't transfer me again," I said through my tears. "All I want to know is if you're going to foreclose on us."

Thankfully, she responded with compassion. No, they wouldn't foreclose as long as we didn't become any more delinquent than we already were. I hung up, somewhat relieved yet drenched in humiliation. I *hated* being in that position. And I hated debt and having unpaid bills. It was a drain on my energy.

And that's when the "little green man," as Vince Pocente calls him, showed up. You know him; he's the one with the Scarcity Voice. Perched on my right shoulder, he hissed, "Jill, are you out of your *mind*? What in the *hell* are you doing? Why are you putting yourself and Steve through this? You're marketable. You could go out and make a solid income. Grow up and just go get a *real* job."

And then, by the grace of God, I heard the Abundancy Voice. "No! Jill, do *not* give this up. This is going to work. You can't give up."

At that very moment I had great clarity. I knew without a doubt that I had to make a choice. I could quit and get a "real" job and my financial stresses would disappear, or I could pick myself up, have faith and recommit.

I chose to recommit.

Perfect Gifts

"The soul won't see what it can't handle."

⌁— AUTHOR UNKNOWN

Grief was new to me when my brother Mike died in 1985. I vividly remember the intense pain as well as the stages of denial, bargaining and anger. I recall driving home to get clothes for his funeral and seeing a child's ball roll onto the street. I felt anger well up in me and I had an irrational, overwhelming urge to speed up and run over that ball. And the next year continued to be a never-ending roller coaster of emotions.

I learned that those stages were necessary in order for me to heal and accept reality. I still mourn the loss of my big brother. I will never forget my love for him, even though I've moved forward.

I also learned that every grief, every loss, has its own schedule. We can't force ourselves to feel emotions just because we know we "should." Sometimes it just takes longer and I had to trust the process.

I learned this again with my youngest brother, Patrick. Although he was eleven years younger, Pat and I were close. Sometimes I felt that he was almost my son. I loved him, as many people did. He had a distinct energy about him that couldn't go unnoticed. He was incredibly handsome but only on rare occasion did I see any arrogance or cockiness in him. He was simply a nice person. People would say, "Oh, my gosh, he's gorgeous! And he's *nice*, too."

Pat enjoyed being outdoors and was physically active. In high school, he was a great basketball and football player and was successful in track, as well. He also enjoyed being in plays and choir.

He was a class act. He had great taste and from the time he was little, he was Mom's "fashion advisor." If she tried something on and Pat didn't like it, she wouldn't buy it. I learned to do the same.

I loved him most for his childlike wackiness. We could be weird together and I could count on him to get the joke when no one else would. His childlike quality was particularly evident when he would give me a big hug when he saw me. Even at twenty-eight years old when he came home with his fiancé, he would holler, "SIS!" and jump on the couch with me for a quick snuggle.

Pat had a heart of gold. He was quick to help someone and rarely said anything bad about anyone. It even showed in his gift-giving. He would give the perfect gift to me or to my mom, because he cared enough to pay attention to who we were.

The most perfect and abundant gift he gave was his last one. He was an organ donor, and when he died on January 4, 1998, at the age of twenty-eight, seven people's lives were saved by his gift.

It was a freakishly cold Saturday morning on January 2 and we were taking our time getting out of our pajamas. The phone rang. It was Dad. He told me that Pat had fallen off an ice arena he was constructing in Mankato, Minnesota. He'd stretched to catch a tool that was thrown to him and slipped off the roof, landing on his head. I was abnormally calm as I heard Dad say, "It's not good, Jill."

Two days later, Pat was pronounced brain dead.

I was numb. I remember walking into the foyer of the funeral home, where nine of my good friends were standing. All of them had tears streaming down their face. I hugged each of them tightly, still without emotion.

"I'm sorry," I said limply. "You're going to have to cry for me. I can't accept this. I won't accept that he's gone."

For a long time, I refused to deal with Pat's death. Two of my three brothers were gone. My family had been ripped from me and I felt like my heart had been as well.

It wasn't until 2004, nearly seven years later, that I finally was able to let go. During my personal retreat, I wrote a letter to the seven people who received Pat's organs when he died.

August 26, 2004

Dear Loved One:

It's approaching seven years since my youngest brother died and I've avoided writing this letter for an equivalent amount of time. Today I know why, as I suppose I've always known. To have written this letter to you would have meant that my baby brother has truly left this world ... and I wasn't ready to say good-bye. Based on the intense pain I'm feeling right now, I'm not sure I'm ready to say good-bye now but I must be nearing a point of closure.

In January of 1998, I openly refused to accept Pat's death. I was in shock. In 1985, our oldest brother had died and he, too, was only 28 years old. At that time, Pat was 16 years old; he never got over it.

My consolation when Pat died was that I had no doubt he would become one of my angels. No matter how fleetingly people knew him, I haven't met anyone who didn't like him. He was a wonderful person ... and I don't think I'm eulogizing him.

I have no idea why I'm blithering on like this. I suppose it's so you know who this person was that entered your life in a very radical way ... and why I've addressed this letter with "Dear Loved One." I cannot help but love you. Pat lives on through you.

Shortly after Pat's death, I was fearful that the transplants may not have been successful. And I was afraid to learn of the outcome. I didn't want to feel the pain of losing him again. Within one year, I believe I received letters from everyone and today I know that regardless of the outcome, he extended lives and the time you had with your loved ones.

It is with deep gratitude that I thank you for giving me the opportunity to express my love of Pat. He's watching over all of us! I pray that you have been blessed with love and health.

With love,

Sis

I've learned that the soul won't see what it can't handle. I was stuck in my denial and grief for a very long time. When I finally took the time to purge and heal I could see that there was a "win"—the gifts Patrick gave to me and to the world.

One Minute at a Time

SERENITY PRAYER

"God grant me serenity
  to accept the things I cannot change,
  courage to change the things I can,
  and wisdom to know the difference."

∾— REINHOLD NEIBUHR

When I was a little girl, Mom had a plaque on the wall above our telephone. It was made of a rich, smooth wood that so fascinated me I gently rubbed it at any opportunity. On the face of the plaque was the Serenity Prayer. Over the years, I must have read that prayer a thousand times. But it didn't become an integral part of my life until I married Steve.

When I met Steve he was a recovering alcoholic, living each day by the grace of God and with the Twelve Steps of the Alcoholics Anonymous program. I became active in Al-Anon and soon learned that the spirit of the Serenity Prayer infuses both AA and Al-Anon; in fact each meeting opens with this moving prayer. I gradually internalized its depth and power and used it as a way to find peace in dealing with every challenge life offered me, personally and professionally. When I become "crazy" I can be assured it's because I've forgotten the Serenity Prayer.

What attracted me to Steve was his quiet warmth and humor, very different from my own extroverted, intense style. He was fairly new to AA; he'd been recovering for more than a year when we met. Steve was thirty-five and I was twenty-five when we married. He was at a point in his life when he was deeply involved in learning about himself, and so was I, so we were at an equal spot in our journey despite our age difference. I admired him for his courage to explore his fears and dreams, no matter how scary or painful they might be. That was probably our tightest bond; we were both eager to be better people.

We were married for thirteen years, and our marriage brought many rich blessings into my life, the best being our son Zach. I won't kid you. It wasn't always easy. Steve was supportive of my business ventures, both Care with Flair and Tastefully Simple, but I'm an all-or-nothing type of person, so when I was trying to grow and run my businesses they consumed much of my time and energy. Understandably, sometimes Steve resented that. It strained our marriage.

Our marriage continued to be tested. In 1996, Steve had sinus surgery which required pain medication. In all the years we'd been together he would never take any prescription drugs. He was committed to his sobriety and was fearful he would slip back into the hellish grips of addiction.

His fears were well founded. Prescription drugs ultimately cost him his life. We separated in early August 1998 and when I took Zach to the house to get his bike on the evening of August 11, I found Steve dead on the floor of our bedroom. He had died from position asphyxia due to over-medication.

Fortunately, Zach was in the living room and I grabbed him as I rushed out the front door in a daze. It was a warm, sunny evening, the sky a bright, clear blue. The memory is freeze-framed. When I got to the front yard I fell to my knees. Complete and utter feelings of resignation, hopelessness, and confusion overwhelmed me.

Looking up to the sky, I asked aloud, "What is your *point*? *What do you WANT from me?*"

My brothers were both dead at twenty-eight, and now Steve. I felt like I was being punished. For the next few days I slipped into survivor mode and felt very little.

It all caught up with me on the night following Steve's funeral. Zach and I were staying at my friend Rose's house, and after I'd put him to bed and turned off the lights, the darkness hit me along with a tidal wave of raw pain, fear and panic. I couldn't breathe.

"He's gone. Steve is gone. Dear God, how am I going to make it through this?" I've learned an important lesson in life over the years: our thoughts control our emotions, and our emotions control our actions. Within seconds I flashed from "Lord, how will I find the strength?" to "How will Zach ever heal from this?" to "How am I going to raise a five-year-old son alone?" to "How will Tastefully Simple survive?"

By the grace of God, those thoughts and the subsequent feelings lasted for only a couple of moments. The next thought I had was, "Jill, you are *not* going to do this one day at a time. You're going to do it one *minute* at a time."

Within a split second, this shift in my thinking allowed me to find peace. I didn't have to know *how* I was going to live through it. I just knew that I would. And it would happen by faith and focusing on the moment, not the future. One *minute* at a time.

Tomorrow's Another Day

"When we walk to the edge of all the light we have
and take that first step into the darkness of the unknown,
we must believe that one of two things will happen:
There will be something solid for us to stand upon,
or, we will be taught how to fly."

— PATRICK OVERTON IN *THE LEANING TREE*

One week after Steve died, Scarlett O'Hara became one of my mentors.

I had only five team members at Headquarters, aka The Shed. One of them was the sales coordinator for our nearly one hundred consultants. She was also helping with setting up conferences, and a ton of other things.

A couple of days after the funeral, she came over to my house. It was a beautiful summer day as we sat on my deck overlooking the back yard. We visited for a while, and eventually she tearfully told me she had decided to go back to her previous job. I didn't blame her. She'd had very little training from me, we were grossly understaffed and she'd had no guidance from me for the past two weeks. We talked about her decision.

I walked her out to her car and gave her a hug good-bye. Mom and my friend Jennie were sitting on the front step, taking a break. They were there helping me get the house and all my personal things in order.

"Well? What happened?" asked Jennie.

"She quit," I said matter-of-factly.

Jennie looked horrified and I knew exactly what she was thinking. Steve had just died, eight months after Patrick. To compound the situation, I was in the middle of moving Tastefully Simple's headquarters from The Shed to a new location. Plus we were just about to hit our first $1,000,000 in sales, and our first regional conference was coming up in two weeks. With a vital team member missing, I was in big trouble.

I looked at Mom and Jennie, and calmly said, "I'm not going to think about it right now. Tomorrow's another day. I'll deal with it on Monday. I'm going to the dry cleaners."

I picked up my cleaning, got in my vehicle, and drove to Hafdal Cleaners.

When I came out of the dry cleaners, an acquaintance, Sue Davidson, was waiting in her car. She got out, gave me a hug, and, without any words, we cried.

Then she said, "Is there anything I can do to help?"

Sue had a background in training and direct sales, and earlier in the year I'd talked to her about working for me. She had declined because she was pursuing other interests. Lightly, I said, "Well, my sales coordinator just quit so the offer is still there if you want a job."

Sue started work two days later.

I learned two significant lessons that day. First, miracles *do* happen. She was a godsend. I truly believe angels brought Sue as a gift.

Second, I had no control of the events of that day. I only had control of how I responded. I was overwhelmed with life at the moment, and to even *think* about what I was going to do felt insurmountable.

There are times when it's difficult to think abundantly. Scarlett O'Hara got the joke when she said, "Tomorrow's another day." She knew how to compartmentalize, put her concerns in a jar, seal the lid, and place it on a shelf to deal with when she felt able.

Get Better or Get Bitter

"It seems not to be a matter of being happy or sad;
it is a new emotion, deeper and more intense than I could have imagined or
can express in words.
The grief is like an inflating balloon, welling up imperceptible over time
until the pin prick of an association bursts the fragile bubble of control."

        — PAULINE STONEHOUSE

Painful things happen to all of us. No one is immune. And it's very difficult to feel abundant and have a win-win outlook when we're in pain.

Why me, we ask?

Why *not* me? Through it all, I've learned my best and most impactful lessons.

First, the best way to let go is to think of something else. That something else was my business. Although the losses and emotional pressures sometimes felt unbearable, Tastefully Simple became my saving grace. Not only was it my financial security with the loss of Steve's income, but it provided me with a way to focus on something other than my personal challenges.

I heard a great life philosophy in Al-Anon: "Get better or get bitter." We can't always choose what happens to us, but we can choose how we respond. I learned that I had a choice. I could become bitter about my lot in life, or I could choose to find something valuable about Steve's and Pat's deaths and get better. I chose better.

Another lesson came from my Grandma Ada, who died suddenly eleven months after Mike died. She was a well-read, deep and philosophical woman. For my twenty-second birthday she gave me two of her books, *Jonathan Livingston Seagull* and *The Prophet* by Kahlil Gibran. For my twenty-fourth birthday she gave me a porcelain bowl made by my cousin Roxy. The Gibran message on it read, "Our joy is our sorrow unmasked." I didn't get it—I didn't fully understand what it meant at the time.

I get it today. We feel our *joy* with the same intensity we've felt *pain*. Now I feel emotions differently. My tears come from deep within. My laughter comes from deep within. I *feel* from deep within. I'm comfortable with my tears. They're a blessing; they cleanse and heal me.

I remember how Zach would react to my tears. He didn't see me cry often but if he even sensed I might cry, he'd bend his little head and search my face with his eyes. Cautiously yet firmly he'd say, "Don't cry, Mom." It seemed to make him uncomfortable, and maybe even frighten him a little.

After a year of his warnings, I finally explained my feelings to him. I said, "Zach, we need to cry. It's how we heal. When we cut ourselves, we need to bleed or the cut will get infected. It's the same with tears. Tears help us heal."

Finally, I learned that I was more transparent and felt safer with people who truly felt the pain of my loss.

When Mike died I was working at First American Bank. I'd taken two or three days off, but I've also learned that there's no place of comfort when you're hurting. I didn't want to be at home, and I didn't want to be at work. I didn't want to be alone, and I didn't want to be with people. There was no avoiding the pain no matter where I went, mentally or physically. Wherever I went, there I was.

And it wasn't that people weren't kind and compassionate. They were very kind. They'd stop by my office to express their condolences and I'd talk about it, but I'd remain quite stoic and composed.

And then Rick stopped by. He and Mike had been friends during their teen years. Rick is a kind, gentle person and as soon as he sat down I could feel my emotions welling up. As we visited and reminisced about Mike, the tears started to stream down my face. I knew he understood.

Sharing our pain with others is a blessing. Whenever someone shares their tears with me, I'm *deeply* honored. It means they trust me and they know they're safe with me.

Painful things happen to all of us. No one is immune. And I know that with time, it's possible to find a place in our hearts where we can see the blessing—and know that the pain has resulted in something abundant and *good*.

Annie the Nanny

"Dealing with change is like dancing with a gorilla.
You don't stop when you get tired,
you stop when the gorilla gets tired."

⌐— JOE FLOWERS

Her name wasn't really Annie the Nanny. That was a fun pet name that Zach and I used which reflected how fond we were of her.

When Steve died in 1998, Zach was only five years old. Four months earlier I'd decided to start taking a salary of $30,000 a year from Tastefully Simple and there was no way this income would stretch to cover child care. This was a challenge.

During the week, Zach was in kindergarten or at Young People's Place. In the evenings he would come to the office with me and watch Pokemon movies, or watch the trains go by, or tape shipping boxes. But in order to grow the company I needed to travel and train our consultants and leaders, which meant that at certain times of the year I'd be gone overnight and on weekends.

There aren't many female CEOs around, and it's not because women are less capable than men of running a company. I believe it's because most women aren't willing to make the family sacrifices—and they are big sacrifices that can produce a lot of guilt. Men expect to be providers so I don't think it's viewed to be as much of a sacrifice.

Now, I'm not afraid of accountability, but I don't like guilt. It doesn't get you anywhere. I love my son, and I love my work. Why should I feel guilty for that? And honestly, I've often told him he's better off having me as a working mom. I jokingly tell him that he would have suffered much greater emotional and psychological damage if I'd been a full-time mom. I would have been Mommy Dearest. I have a *huge* admiration for full-time parents. For me it would be the toughest job in the whole wide world!

Because I couldn't afford to hire someone to watch Zach when I was gone, we were forced to rely on the love and support of my friends. They held me up during the days, weeks, months and years following Steve's death.

Travel during the month of March was the heaviest, when I was gone twenty days out of thirty-one. Each week I'd put a note in Zach's backpack with any special instructions along with his next "drop point" like Thursday and Friday at Glenda's, and Saturday at Jennie's, and Sunday at Rose's. It was an overwhelming time in my life. I would have to consistently remind myself of my "one minute at a time" philosophy. By the grace of God, Zach was an independent, resilient child who thrived on variety. Or maybe he had to learn those skills. Regardless, he handled it with very little, if any, complaint.

By 2000, I had increased my pay to $50,000 and I could afford to hire a nanny to look after Zach when I was gone. Enter Annie the Nanny.

At first Zach wasn't keen on the idea of a nanny. "I don't *want* Annie the Nanny," he said. "I want to stay with your friends!"

"I know, Zach. But I want you to have a routine and more structure. As a mom, that's important to me."

"I don't want a routine. I want to stay with your friends. They're *fun*," he pleaded.

But it didn't take him long to adapt. Annie the Nanny was fun too. One evening Zach and I were standing in the foyer, ready to go out the door. I don't recall what we were discussing. I only remember his searing comment.

"I love Ann more than I love you."

Ouch.

He said this in a rather matter-of-fact tone, yet with a look in his eye that told me he was searching for my reaction. Now I'm pretty good at knowing when someone's trying to push my buttons, so I chose not to take Zach's bait. Not missing a beat, I said, "That's really good to hear, Zach. I'm glad you love Ann so much, because you spend a lot of time with her. There's nothing better for a mom to hear. I want you to be with someone you love as much as you love me."

Even though I knew he said it primarily for effect, it stung. My response to him was truthful but I was sad. I talked it through with myself and concluded, "Well, good Lord, Jill. That's what you *want* for him, isn't it? To have someone around him who loves him and he loves in return? It's not a competition. Zach isn't a prize. He can love more than one person."

We never do it alone. And that's a beautiful thing. On the other hand, it means we'll need to share the credit too. That doesn't always feel so good. In this case, down deep I wanted all the credit, all the love. I had to stop and remind myself that there's always enough to go around.

Today I look at my fourteen-year-old, well-adjusted, much-loved son, the one with all those generous "mothers" who took loving care of him. And I'll be eternally grateful for their abundant hearts.

The Journey

CIRCA 1960
Mom, Mike and me at the 'home farm' where I was raised.

CIRCA 1960
My big brother, Mike, and me –
lots of great memories growing up on the farm.

CIRCA 1962
Mike (left), David (right) and me.

CIRCA 1974
My youngest brother, Patrick.

CIRCA 1981
I spent Sundays working for Dad at the Villard Café. I later managed and co-owned the restaurant, which was renamed Jill's Grill.

1989-1994
In 1989, I started "Care with Flair Gifts & Gift Baskets". While promoting my gift baskets at a local holiday crafter's home tour, I offered taste-testing and experienced incredible results. Ultimately, that success became the inspiration for Tastefully Simple.

1994
Patrick, with my son, Zach. Zach was born in 1992 which influenced my decision to sell Care with Flair.

1995

Tastefully Simple was founded on a dream and a shoestring. From 1995–1998, this 1,200-square foot shed with no running water or air conditioning was 'headquarters'. It was located next door to Joani Nielson's home.

1995

During the early years, a pool table sufficed as the packing station.

1995
*The product display at my first Tastefully Simple party on June 15, 1995.
I was a consultant for three years, typically having 6–18 parties per month.*

CIRCA 1997
*Tastefully Simple's
headquarters team
has come a long
way since the shed.
And it all began
with the passion and
dedication of
Dolly Frost (left) and
Joey Peterson (right).
They held their
paychecks when
cash flow
was tight.*

1997

Top Photo:
Twelve consultants attended the first "real" conference, 'Snowballing in '97'.
It was held at Interlachen Lodge, a rented townhouse in Alexandria.

Bottom Photo:
We don't do it alone. Our HQ team and consultants live our principles every day.
Without them, Tastefully Simple is nothing.

1997
*Joani Nielson, Founding Partner.
Her confidence in the concept of
Tastefully Simple inspired me. She joined
our team as part-time Vice President in 1999
and in 2000, became our full-time
Chief Operating Officer.*

1997
*Dolly, Joey, Linda
and I had a half-day
retreat to create
our core values.*

1998
*The entire
HQ team
in a packing station
(no pool table!) at our
second location on
Nokomis Street.*

2000
*"Papa John" and me
at the
Ernst & Young
award celebration
in Minneapolis.*

2003
*The original
Bungalow Bash Gang
and IQ Group.*

2004
National Conference at the Minneapolis Convention Center -
a far cry from "Snowballing in '97" conference.

2005
Tastefully Simple headquarters located on a 79-acre site
in Alexandria, Minnesota.

2006
Joani and me.

2006
Great things happen only through an amazing team. More than
300 headquarters team members bring their talents to work each day.

2006
My mom,
Jean Schmitz.
She's
'tastefully simple'.

2006
Zachary Michael Blashack.
He always makes me smile.

2006
Gary & I were married
on May 19, 2006
in Austin, Texas.
I thank God every single day
for bringing him to me.
He's the love of my life.

TASTEFULLY SIMPLE®

Core Values

We are committed to exceptional quality, simplicity and uniqueness.

We strive to earn long-term respect and confidence by exceeding expectations.

We are distinctive in our attitude of passion, sincerity and respectfulness.

We celebrate with a cooperative spirit of teamwork and fun.

We nurture the community in which we live.

We are intuitively aware of new products, people and places.

We enrich the lives of our consultants and HQ team members through empowerment and personal development.

chapter three

Make Magic

The Law of Magic

creating positive energy through
celebration and excellence.

Make Magic

*"When we're joyful and we celebrate, magic follows.
When we achieve excellence, magic follows."*

— JILL BLASHACK STRAHAN

We make our own magic in life. And when the Law of Magic is in full force, all feels right with the world.

People are instinctively drawn to great energy. We see a big party going on at the table next to us. They're laughing and energized and connected. And there's a part of us that's thinking, "Dang, I wish I were part of *that* group. They're having a great time!"

People are also instinctively drawn to energy that's created when they're experiencing excellence. And I don't mean stuffy, pretentious excellence. I mean things like an exceptional piece of music, a superb slice of pizza, a beautiful home, a fine car, Disney World. And there's a part of us that's thinking, "Dang, I wish I were part of making *that* happen!"

For me, striving for excellence has always been an expectation. Mom had high standards and I always wanted to do my best. When I didn't, I would become very self-critical. Dad was a driver and expected us to give everything our all.

Celebration, on the other hand, didn't come as naturally for me. How could it? I was focused on what I could have done better. We grew up working. There was no time for that nonsense. When it came to socializing, though, I reigned supreme. I was always up for a few laughs and a good party. I can't tell you how many times I had to write on the blackboard, "I will not talk in class. I will not talk in class. I will not talk in class…"

It sounds a bit odd, but I've learned that I need to be intentional about celebrating. I need to *look* for reasons to honor what's right with the world. We might have a party or we might do the wave — or we might simply give someone a quiet pat on the back and whisper, "Good job!"

And why does all this create wonderful energy? Because we're having *fun* while we're working hard to produce amazing results. In this section I'll share some of my experiences that helped me learn the vital lessons of celebration and excellence.

What magic is

Passion

Good vibes

Synergy

Throwing Koosh balls

Spontaneity

Asking "What's working?"

Attention to details

Under-promising and over-delivering

Least to most

Defining expectations and processes

What magic is not

Negativity

Criticizing

Ignoring good behavior

Complacency

Taking things for granted

Mediocrity

Settling

Slipshod work

Taking the easier, softer way

Change for Change's Sake

"I don't know the key to success,
but the key to failure is trying to please everybody."

— AUTHOR UNKNOWN

When I was twenty-three years old I lived in my hometown of Villard, Minnesota, and, along with Dad, I owned Jill's Grill. It was a typical small town café: old, borderline dilapidated but with a *lot* of character. I only made $400 a month, so in order to make ends meet, I lived in an apartment above the café. It too was old and borderline dilapidated and had a *lot* of character.

I had almost no furniture. In the living room the Sony stereo that I'd bought with my high school graduation money sat on a lovely pressed-wood entertainment center. I had a wicker chair that was a bit lopsided, a wicker chest with a lamp on it, and finally, there was my couch, which was a twin-sized mattress and box spring sitting on the floor. Of course it had an attractive throw over it and a couple of oversized decorator pillows. I'm sure no one *ever* guessed that it was really a bed.

One day someone told me that I should rearrange my quaint living room (all four pieces of furniture.) Now, humble though it was, I thought my living room looked pretty good. But I made a conscious effort to be open-minded, and I asked the fatal question: "How do you think I should change it?"

He proceeded to tell me. When he was done … well, I wasn't sure exactly how to tell him. Frankly, I didn't *like* his vision. He thought all four furniture pieces should be on the same side of the room.

But, still trying to be open-minded and seek to understand, I asked, "Wouldn't the room look a little lopsided that way?"

"Well, maybe," he answered. "But don't you think it would be nice to have a *change*?"

At that instant I had a moment of clarity. I knew that I didn't believe in that philosophy. Yes, change can give us an opportunity to see things from a new perspective, but moving the furniture just to move the furniture was a waste of time and energy.

I explained to him that I believed that change should result in an *improvement*, not just be change for the sake of change.

Sun Studio

"There is an infinite difference between a little wrong and just right,
between fairly good and the best,
between mediocrity and superiority."

⌐— Orison Swett Marden

Jan Strauss had high standards and she knew how to make it a differentiator.

In 1984 I decided to move to Alexandria and leave Jill's Grill. The only challenge was that I didn't have a job. Oops!

I only made $400 a month, which obviously didn't allow for a savings account. In spite of that I looked for a place to live and pursued a personal loan to get an apartment. My goal was to move by April 1. I decided I would move even if didn't have a job. I'd create a position somewhere if I had to. (Okay, so I was a *little* delusional.)

It was a frustrating time. I was clear about what I wanted and was determined to make it happen. Unfortunately, God didn't have the same plan.

I struggled securing an apartment. I'd find something I liked, I'd call them back the next morning, and they'd have rented it.

I struggled getting a loan. Glenwood State Bank didn't seem to appreciate the idea of using my personal belongings as collateral. Can you imagine *that*?! The audacity! Couldn't they see the value in my four pieces of furniture? And no, I wasn't okay with having a co-signer on my loan. I was twenty-four years old and I was *not* going to ask my mom for help.

After two weeks of hitting numerous walls, I stood in my shower, totally spent. I felt powerless. Looking up, with the spraying water streaming down my face, I started crying. "I give up! What do you *want* from me? What do you want me to do? Am I supposed to stay here and not move?"

There was no response.

But somehow I felt better. I'd done all I could, and even though it was in sheer desperation, I turned it over to God. I felt more centered and at peace.

The next day, I found an apartment. It wasn't located in the area that I was hoping for, but I liked it. And I could move in immediately.

Plus I got the loan — although I had to swallow my pride and have Mom co-sign. Sometimes we do what we have to do.

April 1 was moving day. I remember feeling a bit stressed that morning because I still didn't have a job. I convinced myself to have faith.

We were down to the last couple of loads, and as I was about to unplug the telephone, it rang. It was Jan Strauss. She was a teacher at Villard High School. When I was in school I'd been the editor of the school newspaper and Jan had been my advisor. We'd come to know each other quite well.

"Jill, I know you're moving but can you meet me at school? I'd like to talk to you about something."

I was extremely curious. Jan wouldn't be calling me on a whim. So I went.

We sat in the car and she shared her idea. She wanted to start a tanning salon in Alexandria. Would I be interested in helping with the start-up and then managing it for her?

I was stunned. I told her I was flattered and that I'd think about it. I'd never used a tanning bed and I knew nothing about the business. I was also thinking that this couldn't be real. It was too easy. I was prepared for a long job search. It was just too darn easy.

I thought about it for a few days and then called her to say yes. I had a great deal of respect for Jan and her family. I knew she'd do it right and make it a success. Her dad, Arnold Tank, was an excellent businessman and had mentored me when he'd come into Jill's Grill for lunch. He was one of my angels.

It was one of the best things I ever did. I started creating the business plan on April 15 and we opened Sun Studio on June 15. (Oh, and remember the apartment I'd rented? It was right across the street from Sun Studio!)

Tanning beds were still a novelty in 1984 so there was only one other tanning business in town. I needed to know what we would offer that they didn't offer. Jan knew exactly: a new building, cooler rooms, a nice vanity area, bigger tanning beds with timers on them, headsets with music, fresh towels and superb service.

And what would we charge, I asked?

The competition charged $5 per tan. We'd charge $6.

I was concerned. Would the market bear that price? Alexandria is a conservative community. Jan was convinced they would. People would be willing to pay for an excellent experience and great service.

She was right. In the business plan I'd projected we needed thirty people a day to break even. And we were opening in mid-June. Had our *brains* fallen out?! Cash flow was tight in the beginning but on our peak day, eight months later, we had up to 110 people in a day. And that was with only four tanning beds. I would work from 7:30 A.M. to 10 P.M. to get everyone in who wanted an appointment.

Jan was the queen of excellence. She was very particular about the services we offered as well as the ambiance. She wanted a casual, uncluttered environment with warm woods, plants, music, a futon and director's chairs. We greeted everyone as soon as they came in the door and we escorted them to their room. Additionally, she was conscious of our budget and getting the most out of her dollar.

Jan knew about excellence. She knew how to make magic.

Refueling

"Ahhh … too busy driving to stop and get gas?"

᠆ STEPHEN COVEY

I'm a pretty high-energy person. I was blessed with parents and grandparents who could run circles around me. As I said earlier, growing up on a dairy farm we didn't take vacations. And it was okay because we were no different than most of the other farm families.

The guilt that resulted from playing sometimes didn't feel worth it. When I was a teenager, I remember hiding in the ditch if Dad drove by in the afternoon and I was going to the beach to swim with my friends. Once I was an adult, I took great pride in working hard and not taking time off. It was a sign of strength, stamina and work ethic.

I've learned a few lessons that have dramatically changed my attitude.

First, I've learned that not taking time to rejuvenate is a great way to be a martyr. "Oh, absolutely not! I can't go on *vacation.* I'm *way* too busy to take time off!"

Second, what isn't scheduled doesn't happen. It was a big Aha! moment for me when I realized that I had to schedule time to renew. It had to be intentional.

I was at a retreat in 1985 at Blue Cloud Abbey in Marvin, South Dakota, where the facilitator gave us a written "stress test." It contained a number of yes-or-no questions. Have you moved recently? Have you had a death in the family within the past twelve months? Have you recently gotten married? Have you changed jobs in the past year? The list went on. At the end, we had a stress score. If we had over 300 points, we were in the danger zone.

I had 315 points. Within the previous four months, I'd changed jobs, I'd moved, Mike had died, and Steve and I had gotten married. And doing the test didn't help. Seeing the *results* stressed me!

Then she had us list fifty things that we loved doing, things that gave us great pleasure, whatever that might be. I was a good girl and made my list.

Dancing, listening to music, being with friends, watching a beautiful sunset, reading, playing piano, etc.

Next she instructed us to take out our calendar and schedule at least two hours in the upcoming week to do something on our "favorite things" list.

I screwed up my face, looking at her in a bewildered and maybe even disgusted way. I looked at all my friends. They seemed unaffected, quietly and compliantly executing her instructions.

I thought, "This is ridiculous. I'm not going to *schedule* a time to play the piano. It's insane."

I sat back in my chair, resolute. I refuse to do this. But for once I kept my thoughts to myself.

And then I began my internal conversation. "Jill, what's up? Why are you resisting this so much? No one else seems to object. What makes you so special? Why are you willing to fill your calendar with commitments, but you won't schedule time for yourself? Grow up and just do it."

I was right. (And I love it when that happens.) I was the one being ridiculous. So I did it. I scheduled time within the next week to play the piano and read. I was totally out of my comfort zone, but the important thing was that I did it.

Often the difficulty is finding the time to refuel. And I've learned that we never "find" the time. We *make* the time.

The third lesson learned was more painful. Once I discovered how fleeting life was, I had an increased appreciation for and desire to spend more time with the people I loved. After losing two of my brothers and my husband, it was much more important for me to make time for Zach, my family and my friends.

Lastly I learned that when I don't take time for a vacation my attitude starts to deteriorate. I get a little "edgy." (Just ask the people around me!) I lose some of my enthusiasm. I don't have as much oomph. My dreams start to fade a bit, growing a thin, greasy film over them. When I extract myself from my work, when I take time to play and refill my bucket, I'm more productive. I'm more focused and efficient, I'm more fulfilled, and I'm happier.

I go on vacation at least four weeks a year now. And I've had to discipline myself to not bring work along or listen to voice mails or check e-mails. That's been a tough one, mostly for my ego. What do you mean the team can function *without* me? That hurt. But not for long. I'm way over it now.

When I refuel it's an investment in me. It's an investment in being excellent rather than mediocre.

Bungalow Bash

"If you don't take control of your life,
don't complain when others do."

— BETH MENDE CONNY

It was 10:30 at night on my thirty-fifth birthday and I was feeling sorry for myself.

Steve wasn't one to plan festivities, plus with a December 23 birthday I wasn't much in the mood to go out and celebrate anyway. My gala event was wrapping Christmas presents on the living room floor while I watched reruns of "Cheers" on TV and ate cold Pizza Hut pizza.

I have to say, though, I was impressed with my behavior. I wasn't pouting or giving Steve the silent treatment as I'd sometimes done in the past. Instead I was having a little conversation with myself. "Okay. Don't be a baby and act like a victim. So Steve didn't plan anything. There's nothing you can do about that. Plan your own party. Your birthday's at a lousy time of the year, so just celebrate at a different time. Maybe you can have a six-month celebration in June. Or how about having a party in March? March can be a boring month. There are no big holidays and everyone is sick of winter. A party would give people something to look forward to."

And so the decision was made. I would have a birthday party in March. But I wouldn't tell anyone it was a birthday party. It would be my own little secret. I would be the only one who knew that I was throwing a party for *myself*.

New Year's Day rolled around and I started thinking about my goals for 1993. When Mike died in 1985 I had implemented a tradition of asking myself this question each New Year's Day: "What would I do if I only had six months left to live?"

I pondered that question and I concluded that I wasn't having enough fun. My "fun" was my work. What could I do to have more fun? I didn't have any hobbies. So what had been enjoyable for me as a teenager?

Slumber parties! I'd been the queen of slumber parties in the Seventies. Geez, we had so much fun and so many laughs. *I would have a slumber party for my birthday!*

Now I needed to decide who to invite. I was a member of Alexandria's Business and Professional Women, an organization for working women that provides career resources and professional connections. A couple of people in that group were friends: Lou Ann, Glennie, Jennie and Cheryl. Others I knew and admired but hadn't built a friendship with, like Stella, Theresa, Sue and Rose.

So I decided to take a risk. I rented a townhouse at Lake Carlos Villas and invited nine women from that BPW group to my slumber party called the "Bungalow Bash." I was nervous. What if they weren't interested in a friendship with me? What if they thought a slumber party was silly? What if our personalities clashed and the party was a giant flop? One of my requirements was that we all had to stay up all night. What if they didn't *want* to stay up all night? And we had to wear "pie pants," as my friend Wanda called them. You know. They're pants with an elastic waistband so you always have room for pie. Maybe they wouldn't think that was funny!

But the risk paid off. None of those things happened. We all had a fabulous time. We connected, just like you're supposed to do at a good party. We ate tons. We played charades and Pictionary and Truth or Dare. A few of us even "snuck out" at 5 A.M., dodging behind trees and hiding in the shadows. We laughed until we peed our pie pants!

Our buckets were filled. And the Bungalow Bash continues to be an annual event.

Sometimes we have to make our own magic and celebrate.

What Have Been Your Victories?

"When we have hope for the future,
that gives us power in the present."

— JOHN MAXWELL

"Jill? Mike Haynie! What have been your victories?!"

Geez, you'll never know much I hated hearing that question. It was 1994 and every Wednesday morning at 10:30 this was Mike's greeting as I answered the phone for our weekly coaching call.

And so you ask, "Gosh, Jill. You seem a little edgy. Why on earth did you hate this so much?"

That's a very good question, and I took me several years to answer it. Mike grated on my nerves and I wasn't sure why. He was brilliant and was a super nice guy.

The reason: it wasn't him. It was *me*. I wasn't prepared to answer him. Oh, don't get me wrong. I prepared for each of his calls; I was going to make this program worth my time and money. But what I prepared was my litany of all the things I *hadn't* accomplished during the week. I was perfectly prepared with my justifications about why I hadn't achieved all of my goals.

But he never wanted to hear about *those*. Instead he wanted to talk about what I'd gotten done, what I'd accomplished, the "victories" I'd had. It irritated the heck out of me.

And that was what I had to dissect and examine. As I drilled deeper to find the source of my irritation, I realized that I'd spent my entire life kicking myself for what I hadn't done, or what I hadn't done well enough. I was my own best critic and it was the one thing in which I was well disciplined. Regimented self-reprimanding … ooooo, I was good at that. Critical thoughts could just ooze from my head to my heart, almost without solicitation.

So what did this Haynie guy think he was doing? He was messin' with my regimen and it was ticking me off.

Mike taught me a huge lesson, albeit my learning curve took several years. I can choose what I build my life on. I can build it upon my failures, or I can build it upon my successes. If I focus on scarcity and what I don't have, what I haven't accomplished, and where I've failed, that's exactly what I'll continue to spit out in the future. Mike was pushing me out of my comfort zone by forcing me to look for my strengths rather than my weaknesses. Focusing on my victories and my strengths built my confidence and gave me hope. And we become stronger only if we build on our strengths

Over the years, this lesson inspired me to do things differently. At every Tastefully Simple meeting, we open with "What have been your victories?" At dinner each night, we ask each other what our greatest blessing was that day. At the end of each year, I review my list of victories before I begin setting my goals. On the first day of my personal retreat every August I review the victories I've had so far in the year and I write down each and every one. If that nagging little voice surfaces, saying things like, "Here it is August already and you haven't done blah-blah-blah," I show it my list. That's usually enough to shut it up.

Looking for what I've done that's *right* and reflecting on my victories is celebrating the simple, day-to-day things. And that gives me power.

IQ Gang

"We are the average of the five people we spend the most time with."

℃— Jim Rohn

My twelve-week coaching program ended in June 1994, and I missed the accountability that Mike Haynie had provided me. As much as I hate to admit it, I even missed hearing, "Jill! Mike Haynie! What have been your victories?!"

In September, my friend Sue and I attended a personal development retreat sponsored by the Minnesota Business and Professional Women. One of the exercises was to buddy up with someone and talk about our goals. It was great. Sue and I sat by the lake and had a stimulating conversation, sharing what was most important to us, personally and professionally.

On the drive home, we talked about the value of the weekend and how our buckets were filled. And we looked for ways we could maintain the momentum. We needed accountability for the goals we'd set on the shores of Lake Bemidji.

So we came up with an idea. We could form a group of women to meet every couple of weeks, discuss our goals and support each other. It would give us the accountability we were looking for.

But we'd have to find people we could trust. We'd be baring our souls, so confidentiality was imperative. We tossed around some ideas of whom to include. And the more we talked the more it became clear that the Bungalow Bash group could be the answer. The nine of us had had two slumber parties so far and we'd already developed a high trust level. Sue and I instinctively knew this was the right answer.

The nine of us met two weeks later. After much brainstorming we named ourselves InterQuest (IQ), defined our mission statement and established a few guidelines. Our mission statement reads:

"IQ provides a safe environment for focus on individual goals and dreams through support, encouragement and accountability. This connection will serve as an impetus for personal and professional growth."

We each committed to writing our goals and recording our progress in the seven areas coached within the Over the Top program: physical, mental, spiritual, family, social, career and financial.

Our most important guideline was that everything we shared would be held in strictest confidence, because as Stephen Covey says, "The speed of trust exceeds any other speed."

My IQ friends have been a priceless gift. We listen to each other's dreams. We ask the tough questions. We challenge each other to think. We applaud each other's successes, although sometimes half-heartedly if they've just been *too* darn victorious!

These nine women have helped me through pain and tragedy, including the deaths of Steve and Patrick. They've helped me sort through the clutter in my mind and find solutions to countless challenges during the growth of Tastefully Simple. Without them, I may have given up at times when it just seemed too overwhelming. Fear and confusion lose power once spoken aloud.

They've taught me that nothing, and I mean nothing, is out of reach for us. I remember Stella sharing her goal of wanting to be an attorney. Someone in the group said, "Stella, do you realize that you're going to be fifty years old when you graduate from law school?"

In true Stella fashion, she didn't miss a beat. "Well, either way I'm going to be fifty. I may as well as be an attorney."

And she did it. I'm not sure who was more proud: her or *us*! To celebrate we all helped pay for her flight to Florida and stayed at our Tastefully Simple condo for a four-day weekend. That annual trip has also become a fall tradition and is now referred to as our "Enlightenment Conference." If we have to, we make up something we can celebrate — and we always find it!

With the right people around us — people who share our values and strive for making the most out of life — we can effect *huge* change in our lives. They'll hold us up when we're weak, and throw us in the air when we're victorious. And we trust that they'll be there to catch us!

Company's Coming

*"You're gonna do something differently
when you're being world famous than you are
if you're being impatient."*

⌐— FISH! VIDEO © CHARTHOUSE
LEARNING INTERNATIONAL CORPORATION

I couldn't start a company without a name. It made printing the product labels and catalogs a *little* difficult.

So when the concept of taste-testing at home parties occurred to me, one of the first things I needed was a name for the new baby. Joani and I brainstormed names while we dipped Reindeer Chips at Country Kitchen. As the almond bark melted we'd sit in one of the booths, tossing out countless ideas, often laughing until we thought we'd throw up: Yuppy Yum Yums, Chow Hound, Belch and Burp, Little of Dish and Dash, Stark Craving Mad, Purple Cow Gourmet. You see what 2 A.M. brainstorming gets you?

Eventually, we landed on the perfect name. Company's Coming. What a *great* name. We were so proud of our creativity and originality. Then I did a trademark search. Twenty-six companies had trademarked the same name.

Dang! I hate it when that happens. I guess we weren't so brilliant after all.

Now the impact of this wasn't just emotional. It put the brakes on moving forward with many parts of the business. But we couldn't come up with a name we liked as well as Company's Coming. I wasn't just dating that name, I was *married* to it. And the divorce was out of my control.

Joani and I were done with the Reindeer Chip project, so our late-night brainstorming sessions were over. For three months I was at a stalemate as I considered this name and that name. Nothing seemed right. There were some that weren't as bad. Some were "all right" (meaning ho-hum) and I suppose I could have lived with them if I had to. But I *didn't* have to. Details, like names, are an important part of creating excellence. Words have great power, and a name is the foundation of marketing. I knew I couldn't rush it. The name had to be right.

But boy, I got impatient. I was sometimes tempted to slap an "it'll do" name on the company and get on with it. Yet if I was going to settle for less than excellence at the very beginning, I might as well give up now.

Then one day, after three months had gone by, I suddenly remembered something Mom used to say whenever she saw something she thought was classy and elegant. She would say that it was "tastefully simple." Maybe it was how someone dressed. Maybe it was someone's décor. Maybe it was the design of a building.

And I knew that was it. *That* was the name I'd been looking for. It described exactly what we were offering. Excellent taste, with *simple* preparation. Tastefully Simple. It felt right. And the rest, as they say, is history.

In hindsight, I know that Tastefully Simple is not a perfect name. It's a little complex, and I've heard it called "Simply Tasteful" and even "Tastefully Sinful." But Company's Coming? OMG. I thank God that those trademarks existed and I couldn't use the name. We're about enjoying good food *every* day, not just when company's coming. What were we thinking?

The difficulties I experienced in naming the company taught me that excellence takes time. It still may not be perfect but it has to feel right to *you*. It doesn't occur overnight, and it may take longer than you think it should. But if you settle for less, less is what you'll get.

Striving for excellence gives us two wonderful things. One is distinctive quality. The other is patience.

One by One by One

*"I once complained to my father
  that I didn't seem to be able to do things the same way other people did.
  Dad's advice?
  'Margo, don't be a sheep. People hate sheep. They eat sheep.'"*

— MARGO KAUFMAN

In 2006 Tastefully Simple reached $120 million in sales. When I stop and think about those sales, it seems surreal.

When creating the business plan in 1995, I was conservative. I projected we'd have average sales of at least $300 per party: attendance of twelve people per party and a $25 average purchase. I'd also determined that there were two primary things that could threaten the success of Tastefully Simple.

The first threat was that the products were targeted to busy women. Tupperware parties had been ragingly successful in their day due to their excellent products, yet it was during a time when many women weren't working outside the home. They used the parties as a social venue. Would women be too *busy* to come to a Tastefully Simple party? Attendance was critical; I knew once people tasted the products they'd be jazzed.

The second threat was that the average price point was $5.95. Would guests come to the party and buy one product as a "pity purchase?" And I was starting with only twenty-two products in the catalog. If they were the wrong products, my odds were higher that I'd get the pity purchase.

In addition, my home party business skills were — well, they were quite unimpressive. I didn't know how to book a party. I didn't know how to build and train a team. I had limited product knowledge. But I didn't classify this as a threat. I knew I would acquire those skills as I went along, through trial and error and by learning from others.

I concluded the threats were real but the risk was worth it. Plus, as Tanya Roufs, consultant #0000002, later eloquently said, "It isn't like we have a trunk full of toothbrushes. It's *food!*"

So I plunged in and had my first Tastefully Simple party on June 15, 1995. It was a fabulous spring evening. When I came driving up to The Shed, Joani bounded out of her house (she always looks so darn *cute*) and ran up to my little blue Grand Am.

"*Well?* How did it go?"

I hesitated as I gathered my summary thoughts. "I have good news and bad news. The bad news is that there were just five buying guests at the party and the sales were only $200."

Okay. Threat #1 looming large. If guests didn't come to the party we were sunk. After my costs, this $200 party would yield approximately $40 in income, or roughly $8 per hour. It would be unlikely our sales consultants would be pumped about that income.

"But the *good* news," I continued, "is that four out of the five guests booked a party. And the average purchase was $40 per person, not $25."

Bingo! *That* was exciting. It meant they loved the concept of our parties, and the product mix was right. I know. Clearly this was a pathetically small market sampling. The best way to see if it would work was to get my butt out there and do more parties.

My fears were unfounded. People were enthralled with the parties—they were fun, they were social and they were non-threatening because everyone just sat around eating and experiencing the products. Who wouldn't want to come to *that* party?

Average sales at my subsequent parties were $400 and my fourth quarter averages went up to $600 per party.

Now, were they *all* like that? Well, no. I did I have a $49 party too.

Lesson learned? Don't let your dad have a party. And if you do let your dad have a party, coach him like you would any host. It was *my* fault that I heard myself saying, "Um, Dad? Those invitations were supposed to be *mailed*." Thank goodness his cousin Winkie happened to stop by so he got a $49 order! (When I think about it more, he may have had the party just to get on my schedule.)

Seriously, bless Dad's heart for even *offering* to have a party. How many dads would do that? He was one of my biggest supporters. He had total faith in me. What a gift. He died in November 2005 and I miss him deeply. I still feel wrapped in his love and faith though. That will never leave me.

So, yes. I had parties with low sales. On the other hand, did I have a $2,000 party? Absolutely!

Lesson learned? No one party will make or break your business. You take it all. It's a package deal. On rare occasions, I lost money doing a party. On rare occasions, I earned $400 per party.

The success of Tastefully Simple is an overwhelming testimonial to the power of one. We build things one by one by one: one decision at a time, one fear at a time, one sale at a time, one relationship at a time.

That's a Spoon

"Celebrate what you want to see more of."

— Tom Peters

Sometimes we set out to teach someone something, and we end up learning as much as they do.

Years ago, when Zach was around five years old and Tastefully Simple was two, Joani popped out to The Shed to visit. As we were chatting about our kids, she shared something she'd learned in a parenting magazine. It was a non-reactive, non-judgmental technique for teaching good behavior to children. I was impressed with the technique, and immediately decided to give it a try.

I put a drinking glass on top of the refrigerator — glass, not plastic. Whenever Zach did something that was an infraction of the rules, or if he had inappropriate behavior, he would get a spoon. (No, I didn't beat him with it!) I would open the silverware drawer and put the spoon into the glass, making sure it made a tinkling sound. Sound effect is very important.

The rule is, if you have to tell the "perpetrator" more than one time to do whatever it is they're supposed to do, or to stop their inappropriate behavior, they get a spoon in the glass. For instance, if Zach wasn't sharing his toys with a friend, or if I had to remind him to make his bed, I would merely get a spoon and put it in the glass. Tinkle, tinkle. (Sound effect.) I don't get mad. I don't make a big scene. I simply put a spoon in the glass. Once there are six spoons in the glass, there's a consequence. Perhaps he can't go to his friend's house overnight. Or maybe he can't go to a birthday party. It needs to be a sizeable consequence.

This was a great technique that got even better because Zach could redeem himself through good behavior. When he did something well, I would take a spoon *out* of the glass.

One morning Zach must have gotten up on the wrong side of the bed. I swear, between the time I brushed my teeth and put on my mascara, I had given him four spoons. (*Lots* of sound effect.) He was on a roll — and it wasn't a good roll. When I brought him to Young People's Place that morning, he had a total of five spoons looming large in his glass. One more and he would have a consequence.

Now, if you're a parent, do you *like* giving your child consequences? I didn't think so. Most of us don't like to punish our kids. It's not the fun part of being a parent. So what do you suppose I did when we got home that night? Zach had five spoons, and I started to look for things that he was doing *right* so I could take a spoon out of the glass.

I saw my opportunity.

"Way to go, Zach. You cleared your plate without me asking!"

His little face beamed as he saw me take a spoon out of his glass.

And then an amazing thing took place. He began scurrying around looking for more things he could do right. He cleared the rest of the table, he helped dry the dishes, he said please and thank you. The spoons were coming out of the glass nearly as fast as they'd gone in.

I believe it's human nature to see what's missing or what's wrong with the world. Zach's response was also human nature. We all like to be recognized for what we're doing right, for our *good* behavior. It was a "Duh!" moment for me. Again, it's better to build on the rock foundation of someone's strength rather than on the sands of their weakness. We'll never become better people by building on our character *defects*.

Lesson learned: *Celebrate* what I want to see more of and more of it will appear.

Pizza and Movie Night

"You can have anything you want in life.
You just can't have everything."

— PETER MCWILLIAMS

Here's a hard truth: when we say *yes* to something, we're saying *no* to something else. We don't have infinite space and infinite time. We must make choices. Actually, we have no choice about making choices, which sounds like a contradiction but isn't. We choose by intention, or we choose by inattention.

The results of our choices are what make up our life. I'd always been imbalanced when it came to my choices, leaning heavily toward my work. That's because my choices weren't always *intentional* choices. If left to my own natural leanings, I would always choose career health over physical health, for example. I had to learn to make conscious choices to keep my life from tilting out of balance.

One of my best teachers in this arena has been my son, Zach. Somewhere around the age of eight, when he was in second grade, he started to resent my work. One evening after we'd left Tastefully Simple, he launched into a very convincing sales pitch that lasted about twenty minutes. He was explaining to me that he thought I shouldn't work so much.

"Well, how much do you think I should be working, Honey?"

One day a week, he thought. And probably Friday. Yeah, Friday would be a good day to work.

A bit amused, I listened, asking questions to better understand and perhaps get him to shift his thinking! I continued listening as we pulled up to the garage, sitting in my Explorer while we discussed his vision of our life.

"But don't most of your friends' moms work?" I asked, trying to get him to see that he was not the only child with a working mom.

"Lucas' mom doesn't work," he said stubbornly, referring to perhaps the only stay-at-home mom he knew.

"I wonder what his dad does for a living."

He didn't know.

"I think he's an attorney, Honey. Zach, in three years I've never used this as an excuse, but since your dad died, I'm both Mom and Dad. I need to make the house payment and pay for our food and our clothes and our groceries. Thank God we had Tastefully Simple when he died because I didn't have to worry about finding a job."

Zach is very bright and he knows what he wants. So of course nothing I said cut any mustard with him. He clung to the idea that I should become Lucas' mom and continued selling me as we walked into the house. I knew I needed to dispel this vision of his, because it was next to impossible that I'd ever be his dream mom. We were standing in the kitchen when finally I turned to him and said firmly, "Zach. It is what it is. I need to work full time. I won't be working one day a week."

The look on his face is emblazoned in my mind. He looked up at me, eyebrows lifted in alarm, his big hazel eyes incredulously wide, brimming with tears. The full impact of my words hit him.

"You're *not?*"

He ran out of the kitchen, down the hall, into his room, slammed the door, and threw himself on the bed, all the while sobbing.

Sigh.

If you're a parent, I know you've been there.

But I had to admit that he had a valid point. He deserved more of my time, and I wanted to spend more of my time with him. The answer was not to make a vague promise to do better, but to make an intentional choice and set a definite goal to do so.

I once heard a speaker share that when families have high stress, it's because their boundaries are ambiguous. They don't make it clear when they're working and when they're not. For instance, if on Saturday morning a spouse tells their family that they're going into the office "for a while" and then by 3 P.M. they're still not home, this causes a lot of stress and resentment. Nobody knows when they're coming home, or whether or not they should include them in their plans for the rest of their afternoon.

But if they'd said, "Hey, I've got to get this project done today, but I'll be home at noon and we'll go to the matinee," everyone knows what to expect and they can move on with their own lives.

So as a way to create better boundaries and to take time to relax and play together, Zach and I instituted "Pizza & Movie Night." Every Friday night we'd order a pizza and rent a movie from the video store. And we would spend the evening together, just the two of us. It was *our* time.

Now I'm not claiming that pizza and a movie are the be-all and end-all of parenting—especially since I sometimes didn't make it to the end of the movie without falling asleep on the couch! But it was a boundary that we set within our relationship which we both could count on. I had to make a conscious choice to say "yes" to Zach.

The Mind Is a Magnet

"Most of us have been trained to take the lukewarm approach to achieving our goals:
'I'll try it a little bit and see what happens.'
The trouble is, lukewarm commitment generally produces lukewarm results.
Based on the lukewarm results, people often say,
'Well that didn't work out. It's a good thing I didn't commit myself.'
It was, in fact, the lack of commitment that produced lackluster results."

— Peter McWilliams

I've become a goal-setting fanatic. I'd never experienced the power of goal-setting until Mike Haynie convinced me to give it a try. And now I understand that goal-setting is about living with intent and having a life of excellence. It's a tangible way to recognize that life is short and it helps us *choose* how we live.

In 1998, I read *Simple Abundance* by Sarah Ban Breathnach, where I learned how to keep a Discovery Journal. It's a scrapbook filled with pictures, sayings, quotes or representations of things that trip my trigger. Things I want to have in my life. It's visual dreaming. My Discovery Journal has several sections:

Return to Self

Authentic Success

Spiritual Journey

Authentic Style

Entertainment

Relationships

House of Belonging

The "House of Belonging" section was easy for me to start and it filled quickly, earning the right to have its own book. Over a period of three years, I ripped countless photos from magazines. I clipped pictures of homes with warm light spilling into the night air, exteriors rich with stone and chunky beams and lots of windows, many of them log homes. I included shots of twinkling lights in the backyard; a fire pit encircled with friends; landscapes with fountains and abundant foliage and cobblestone pathways. And I'd always dreamed of living on a lake, so those photos were sprinkled throughout.

The interiors included lots of wood — warm, comforting wood. And there were plants and leather furnishings and fireplaces and stone and area rugs with furniture arranged for conversation and "cuddle chairs" instead of the stuffy, uncomfortable, straight-back chairs that made me want to run far and run fast.

During several of those years, I was earning $30,000 to $50,000 a year and was a single mom. I could hardly afford the magazines I tore the pictures from, let alone afford the homes that I was adding to my Discovery Journal. As Tastefully Simple grew and I became more confident about our future, I decided to begin a "soft search" to look for a house on a lake. I wasn't committed to the idea because I didn't like the price tag attached to lake property. Again, my Scarcity Voice was whispering, "Don't over-extend yourself. You and Zach are perfectly happy in the house you have. What happens if you buy a more expensive one and Tastefully Simple doesn't work? You'll lose the house."

I belonged to an international CEO group called "TEC," now called "Vistage," and after much cajoling (aka harassing), they convinced me that I deserved to buy a house on a lake. Tastefully Simple was going to hit nearly $35 million in sales, I was only taking a salary of $50,000, plus I'd been working 60 to 80 hours a week for over five years. I told them that I would consider it but if I did buy a different home, I refused to have a mortgage. Although it wouldn't be smart from a tax perspective, it would be smart from a personal perspective. It was a "sleep level" decision — I would sleep better at night.

In October 2001, Zach and I moved into a 30-year-old log home overlooking a beautiful lake, set on two-and-a-half wooded acres. I felt at home the minute I saw it. It had full-length windows in nearly every room, providing a beautiful view of the lake. It had lots of wood and stone and fireplaces.

And the entire main level had either hardwood floors or Spanish tile. Now if you'd asked me prior to 2001 if my ideal home would have carpeting throughout the house, or hardwood floors and tile, or a combination of both, I would have responded, "A combination of both but predominantly carpet." About a year after we'd moved in, I was thumbing through my House of

Belonging Discovery Journal and I saw something that fascinated me. I had roughly forty-five pictures of interiors of homes and *every photo* had hardwood floors or tile.

Next I saw that one of my Discovery Journal clippings was an advertisement for an outdoor Bose music system. The photo showed a patio party, water in the background and in the foreground two Bose speakers hanging above the patio doors. If you had added some trees in the backyard it would have looked exactly like the view from my kitchen patio doors with Bose speakers over the office patio doors. And those speakers were there when we bought the house. (I promise you: I'm not making this up.)

There are way too many miracle stories from my Discovery Journal to relate all of them here.

And don't get me wrong. With any successful goal-setting we also need to be realistic. If we think that it's going to happen overnight, it's not. As Samuel Goldwyn said, "The harder I work, the luckier I get."

Discovery Journals are about visual goal-setting, dreaming with intent, and allowing the mind and heart to move toward their focus. And it works. The mind is a magnet.

Hats in the Air

"Dream big. Wink often."

— Author Unknown

Monday, June 17, 2000: a historic date for Tastefully Simple.

We were five years old and we'd just moved into our brand-new headquarters. We'd moved from The Shed to the Nokomis Street warehouse, and now we were in our permanent location one mile out of town, set on twenty-two acres next to beautiful woods and wetlands.

Accordingly, we'd invited all thirty of our team members to a little celebration. It was to begin at 9:20 A.M., in honor of our new address, 1920 Turning Leaf Lane. As a gift, I'd purchased Tastefully Simple baseball caps for everyone.

So there we all were, the first day in our new work areas, in our brand-new building. But the mood was anything but celebratory. I mean, think about it. You're in a new space, all your belongings have been moved over the weekend, you can't find your stapler or your favorite pen, you don't know how to use your new phone, and your files are in a cardboard box sitting on the floor. Everyone was just a *little* tense.

At nine o'clock I pulled Joani into my office.

"What was I *thinking*? Am I out of my mind? We can't do this celebration. It's our first day in the new building and everyone's stressed! Maybe we should do it tomorrow."

"But," I continued, after a few more rants, "as Andy Longclaw says in the book *Gung Ho*, recognition must be TRUE — Timely, Responsive, Unconditional and Enthusiastic. We can't wait. We need to have the celebration now."

With Joani's typical patience and composure, she hadn't said a word. She just listened to me rant and rave. She's really good at that. She knows there's no point in arguing with me, since I do such a good job of arguing with myself.

My circular tirade over, at 9:20 I paged everyone in the building to join us outside by the warehouse loading docks. It was a beautiful June day, warm and sunny, with a perfectly clear blue sky.

I gave a little speech about June being the season of graduation, and like high school graduates, this new building was indicative of moving into a new phase of our lives.

We passed out the baseball caps, and in true graduation tradition we all cheered and threw our hats into the air while we sprayed everyone with Silly String. Afterwards, we went into our break room, the "Squirrel's Nest," and had muffins and coffee. The whole celebration took less than half an hour.

But what do you suppose the mood was like at Tastefully Simple after we all got back to our work stations? The tension was "Poof, gone."

Here's what I've learned about myself: When I'm all stressed out with no one to choke, when I'm "in the grip"—that's when I need to take the time to celebrate what's *right* with the world. When I least feel like celebrating is when I most need it.

Picking Fly (Stuff) Out of Pepper

*"It is not given us to live lives of undisrupted calm, boredom and mediocrity.
It is given us to be edge-dwellers."*

— AUTHOR UNKNOWN

I admit it: I drive people crazy. My mom taught me well with her mantra, "Anything worth doing is worth doing well." I strive for excellence and will beat the crap out of something until I believe it's a ten. Some people might even call me fanatical.

Take our Tastefully Simple conferences, for example. Conferences were far from excellent for the first three to four years. I did the majority of the training myself which was, without a doubt, a classic illustration of the blind leading the blind. I was still learning the business along with our consultants. On a positive note, one thing I think I was good at was making the training understandable and interesting.

National Conference was held in Alexandria each year over a three-day weekend. The first year there were twelve consultants there. The third year thirty attended. As much as I wanted to, I knew it wasn't feasible for me to do every speck of the training. But I was too cheap to hire speakers and bring them to the Holiday Inn in Alexandria. Instead I found people who were in the industry, had big hearts and were willing to work for food. Translation: I would give them Tastefully Simple products in exchange for their time. (And I'm sure I reported that on their 1099s.)

I learned and got better as time went on, but as the size of the company grew along with the number of HQ team members, I knew I had to let go more. The team needed to be stretched and I was killing myself with the workload. In 2000 we achieved $11.8 million in sales and it was impossible to do everything. There was no choice but to let people run with their skills and passion.

Regardless, letting go and empowering other people to do the training was very difficult for me. I still attended *every* rehearsal for *every* training. And they were grueling. I'm a zealot about having great presentations. I want the message to be clear and presented in a way that will motivate people to take action. We would spend hours going through the content and the handouts, hearing every minute of the presentation and giving suggestions on how they could be improved. Sometimes it was almost brutal. It's hard to work on a presentation, put your heart and soul into it, and then have people give feedback. Some people take it personally and think we're calling their baby ugly.

Well, one of the National Conference presentations wasn't ready when we had rehearsals. Things were crazy busy, and consequently, I didn't have time to see the presenter rehearse before she went on stage.

By this point we had more than 200 consultants attending National Conference, so we were at the Hilton in Bloomington. I was sitting in the audience with the other consultants as the presenter came on stage and began her session. As each minute ticked by it became painfully clear that it was far from "excellence." She wasn't prepared and the content was confusing. To make matters worse, the information was incorrect. The consultants were looking at each other in confusion, some simply putting their pens down in frustration. I was mortified.

It was a lesson I didn't forget. I hadn't taken the time to ensure excellence.

One year later we were in the Maple Room at HQ, again going through the mental marathon of conference rehearsals. We'd been dissecting one session for the entire day—from 8:00 in the morning until 8:00 at night. It was still not right. It's not that we weren't all working hard. We were. It just needed to be better. Everyone was exhausted, and resentment and animosity were heavy in the room. As we left, I knew I wasn't winning any popularity contests with the team.

It bothered me and I processed it throughout the remainder of the night. What could I do to make the process better? Was I wrong? Was I too demanding?

We were back in the war room at 8 A.M. I could still feel the tension and I knew what I needed to do. As the presenter began, I interrupted.

"Hey, guys. I'm sorry to interrupt but I'd like to talk about yesterday. I know it was a tough day and I've thought a lot about it. I want you to know that I really appreciate all of your hard work and the long hours you've been devoting to this.

"I could feel the tension when we left last night and I'm sure you're not liking me too much right now. You're thinking I'm being a perfectionist and that I'm picking fly (stuff) out of pepper. So I need you to know my philosophy: we can do this here and now at HQ with just the eight of us. Or we can get up on stage in two weeks and let 500 of our consultants do it for us. And they will. They deserve excellence and they expect it. I know this is painful, but the payoff for us will be the feeling we have when we've delivered something excellent to our consultants."

And we did.

We still do, and I no longer attend rehearsals. We devote an immense amount of time and energy to our conferences. As a matter of fact, our threshold goal is to achieve an overall score of 5.5 on a scale of 1 to 6. That's a score between very good and outstanding. It's like saying that we'll settle for an A instead of an A+.

And you know what? We do it. Nearly every single time, we do it. The team is amazing. They have a passion for magic and creating excellence. And they're willing to pick fly (stuff) out of pepper to achieve it.

Start Where You Are

*"You go as far as you can see
and when you get there
you will always be able to see farther."*

— Zig Ziglar

It was a beautiful Saturday morning in July and Zach was staying with friends for a couple of days. I was in heaven. I slept in, I took a walk, I made a pot of coffee, and I had breakfast on the patio. It was glorious!

Before I brought my breakfast outside, I wiped off the water, leaves, dead bugs, and cobwebs from my patio furniture. And suddenly I was inspired. I felt all warm and fuzzy as I remembered buying that patio set several years earlier. I love it and mostly because when I sit there it feels like I've come home. It's a nice Homecrest patio set. You know the kind — a round table with a glass top, an umbrella and four mesh chairs. Sort of a taupe and cream fern pattern. I don't recall how much it cost. Maybe $800 to $1,000, which was a lot of money back in 1996 when Steve and I were living hand-to-mouth.

What inspired me that day on my patio, though, was remembering that I had set a goal to have a patio set. I was struck by the *simplicity* of that goal. I hadn't wanted a new house. I hadn't wanted a fancy car. I hadn't wanted a month-long trip to Europe. I had just wanted a nice patio set.

In 1995 Lori Tiffany became one of my first Tastefully Simple consultants — consultant #0000003. Lori had a goal when she started her business. Her goal was to earn enough "pocket money" to buy two gifts for her husband, Craig, every year. She wanted to be able to spend $50 on him for his birthday and $50 on him at Christmas.

Lori Tiffany became a Senior Team Mentor, eventually achieving a six-digit income, and by the end of 2006 she had team sales of over $8 million. Not only has she been able to buy Craig his Christmas and birthday gifts, they've gone on several family trips and added onto their home, including a third stall in their garage. What more would make a man smile?

Excellence is built one step at a time, one day at a time, one goal at a time. We set a goal that stretches us a little, and once we get there we'll be able to see further. Those modest goals can turn into springboards that catapult us to the next level and the next fulfilled dream.

First an $800 patio set, then maybe a new yard to put it on. First a $50 birthday gift, then maybe a $5,000 charity contribution. Start where you are. The rest will follow.

Divine Discontent

"Water seeks its own level.
Surround yourself with people who hunger to be better
and who want to rise to a whole new level."

— JILL BLASHACK STRAHAN

"I love being with people who have Divine Discontent."

I was speaking at a Tastefully Simple event in Tacoma, Washington, and we were talking about why we liked being involved with Tastefully Simple. That's when Kay Watson, a Tastefully Simple consultant, summed it up with this comment.

I was intrigued. "Divine Discontent." What an absolutely awesome phrase. I, too, love being with people who have Divine Discontent, people who are always looking for ways to improve and are never quite satisfied because they know they can always be better. Joani is one of those people.

Divine Discontent doesn't mean we're unhappy people. Quite the contrary. It's about choosing our attitude and not playing victim to life.

I know. There are people who don't get it. They're the ones who think, "Geez, Jill. Can't you just accept things the way they are?"

Absolutely. If they're things I can't change. Accepting the things we can't change is the key to peace and contentment. Sometimes we have to be willing to lie down in the water and let the current take us where it flows.

When we look for ways to make things better, it's like pushing against something to build a muscle. That creates positive results. Divine Discontent is knowing that there are *so many things* you can change—for the better. Life becomes one big candy store!

Now I understand that this produces some chaos that can drive people nuts. But you have to agree that it's a *creative* chaos that often yields excellent results. Being open to continuous improvement is frequently the differentiator between someone who's good and someone who's great. Great is someone who looks for possibilities. Someone who's divinely discontented.

I dig those people. They kindle the desire for me to be better.

Ideal Man

"The thoughts we feed will be the thoughts that win."

— Author Unknown

I had begun to believe that I was destined to a life without true, romantic love. For several years the thought of totally loving anyone resulted in a feeling of impending doom, fear and pain. I kept losing people I loved. Why on earth would I hang my heart out to be sliced to smithereens again?

I distinctly remember sitting in church in mid-December 2004 saying a prayer. "God, thank you for my wonderful and full life. I'm so blessed. I have a great son, an incredible business, financial security, and the best friends and family in the whole world. I don't expect to have it all. Please grant me peace and serenity to accept my life as it is."

Because of my unrest, I had persisted in the creation of my Discovery Journal—even the Relationships pages. Over several years I accumulated quotes like, "Ever had the feeling you could trust someone all the way down to your toes?" or "The person you can't wait to come home to," or "Why drool on something dull?" Or my favorite, a quote by Linford Detweiler: "The life you are meant to find will wring your heart to the point of breaking—and then douse you with buckets of joy when you're not looking." That one gave me hope.

The photos were of couples snuggling and laughing and walking down Italian streets and boating and holding hands and snuggling. (Did I say that already?) And there was one tiny photo of a couple dancing outdoors—and next to it I placed the clipping, "I dream of meeting a man who can dance."

In 2002 a friend had shared that he'd created a list of all the qualities he'd want in a partner. I liked that idea, so I created a document called "Ideal Man." It had four categories: mental, emotional, physical and financial.

It included traits like a good parent who loves Zach, intelligent, curious, a stimulating conversationalist who makes me think, honest, dependable, committed, supportive, social, respectful, relaxed, fun-loving, compassionate, romantic (he adores me and I adore him), tenacious, positive, self-confident, tall, attractive, healthy, demonstrative hugger who loves to snuggle, high energy and requires little sleep, sexy, passionate, spiritual, humble, non-judgmental, generous and financially secure.

Whew! And this isn't the *whole* list. I was very specific — like to the tune of two pages of characteristics.

On top of that, I set a goal in 2004 that I would meet the man that I was going to marry.

I met Gary Strahan on December 30, 2004, and we were married in Austin, Texas, overlooking Lake Travis on May 19, 2006. I may be blinded by love but I believe he possesses every one of the above qualities, and *more*. He's the love of my life, and I thank God every single day for bringing him to me.

And not only *can* he dance, he *loves* to dance!

Hang Out With the Motors

*"There are two kinds of people, the anchors and the motors.
You want to lose the anchors and get with the motors,
because the motors are going somewhere and they're having more fun.
The anchors will just drag you down."*

— WYLAND, MARINE ARTIST

Excellence is an attitude. It's a way of thinking. Being an anchor is easy. It's our typical behavior whenever we're confronted with something new or difficult.

I'm no exception. I remember when we introduced the "Club 24" challenge at our Leadership Hollywood conference in 2005. We challenged our Tastefully Simple leaders to accept the goal of adding twenty-four people to their team in one year. I have to be honest. When I first heard about this, I had anchor thoughts. "Are we out of our *mind*? How many people are going to accept the challenge of bringing on twenty-four consultants in one year?"

But when we introduced the challenge at the conference, Joy, one of our Team Managers, immediately piped up with, "Oh, I can do that! It's only two new consultants a month!"

Duh! She was so right. I was ashamed of my attitude. Joy is a motor, and hearing her excitement got me charged up, too.

And then I had an Aha! moment. Back in 1997, when I was in the midst of a one-year dry spell in recruiting (yes, one *year*), I went to a Creative Memories conference as a corporate guest. After hanging out with those motors for a couple of days, I came back rejuvenated. I set a goal to recruit eight new consultants in the next four months.

I signed eight consultants in *six weeks*! I recruited someone at nearly every single party.

And do you know why? Because I hung out with the motors, I opened my mind to new thoughts and ideas, I set a goal, and I *believed* I could.

We have a choice. We can talk negatively to ourselves and hang out with the anchors who suck the very life blood right out of us. Or we can spend our time with the motors who infuse us with enthusiasm.

I know what you're thinking: "But what if the anchors are on my team or in my family or are my co-workers? Then what?"

Good point. All of us will be exposed to anchors; they'll appear in every arena of our life, filling our hearts with negative, unproductive, uninspiring whining—"I can't make money in this business," "That's impossible," "They'll never let you do that."

Unfortunately we can't always "lift anchor" and go find another crew. And yet, we still have choices. We can choose to focus our energy on the anchors in our life, or we can focus our energy on the motors. We can choose to limit our exposure to those heavy anchors; we don't have to join them in their favorite game of "Ain't life awful?" We can choose to expand our circle to include more motors so the anchors exert less pull.

We can also choose to have compassion for the anchors. When people are negative, they're usually feeling powerless. When we join them, we're validating their powerlessness. We're agreeing that they have no power to change or grow. The most compassionate and kind way to deal with them is to surround them with motors. They will either become motors themselves, or they will go hang out with other anchors. Let them go with love.

Like my response to Club 24, we'll be our own biggest anchor if we tell ourselves, "I can't do that." And we'll gravitate toward people who hold the same beliefs. On the other hand, like my goal of recruiting eight people, we'll be our own biggest motor when we say, "I can do it!"

Self-Love

"When Mama ain't happy, ain't nobody happy."

— Author Unknown

Every August since 2002, I've scheduled a personal retreat. I go away by myself for two or three nights: Grand Superior Lodge on Lake Superior; Sundara Spa in Wisconsin; Lake Geneva, Wisconsin; Austin, Texas; Madden's Resort in Brainerd.

I review my goals, paying special attention to my victories and achievements. I think about what I've learned and how I can apply those lessons in the future. I take the time to *feel*, whether it's a heart full of gratitude or healing tears. I dream big dreams and little ones. I let myself really see my perfect life. I thank God for the gifts and blessings I've been given and for all the people who've been put in my life. I leave feeling whole and totally filled.

In spite of the huge value of this experience, every August I struggle with going on my retreat. I feel guilty for leaving Zach. I work a lot of hours and have limited time at home. How can I do this? It feels very, very selfish. And I feel sad because I want to be home. I'd rather be at home with Gary and Zach. I love being with them.

Gary and I had been married for only three months when I went on my fifth personal retreat. It was after Tastefully Simple's National Conference so I'd been gone for several days and preparation for the trainings and unveilings had required 80-hour workweeks. I'd returned home from the conference and then left for our Focus Retreat, a three-day strategic planning event. I was exhausted and was deeply longing to just be home, snuggling with Gary and hanging out with Zach.

The day I was to leave was the same day as our Community Live & Learn event. In partnership with the community each year we bring in a top-name speaker: Stephen Covey, Ken Blanchard, Zig Ziglar. This year we were honored to have Jack Canfield. His presentation was a perfect "seed message" for my personal retreat.

Afterwards, I went home, had dinner with Gary and Zach, and packed. And then I stalled. I took my time, I lollygagged, I procrastinated. By 10 P.M. I still wasn't out the door and on my two-hour drive up north. I didn't want to go. I had this intense voice screaming at me to *stay home*. As I stood with the door open, I clung to Gary, crying. Sobbing, actually. "I don't want to go, Gary. I just want to be *home*."

Gary was amazing. I'm nearly certain he was thinking, "Then don't go! Why are you torturing yourself? I don't want you to leave either!" But instead he held me tight, wiped away my tears, looked me in the eye and said, "Go, Sweetie. You need to go."

I knew he was right. Deep in my heart I knew that I was being tested to see how rooted my commitment was. I didn't have to go on the retreat. No one else was counting on me to be there. It was a commitment only to myself. And I needed to honor my commitment to myself as much as I would honor a commitment to anyone else.

So I went. I resisted the overwhelming temptation to renege. And it was worth every tormented tear. Here's an excerpt from what I wrote at the close of that personal retreat:

"I'm packed and ready to head out the door. And what an appropriate ending to my personal retreat as I hear Celine Dion singing, "A new day has come. I've been touched by an angel."

The rain is pattering on the wooden desk and the ducks are oblivious as they float by. I breathe in the smell of pine sap, a bit sad to leave and yet feeling renewed and ready to re-enter the world. I've missed Gary and Zach, and Mom arrived in Alexandria yesterday.

God works in mysterious ways. Jack Canfield spoke on Tuesday and he was my angel. As I watched a DVD he gave me, I was slapped with the realization that I'd lost my focus on dreaming and believing. Oh, I certainly used that miraculous power when I defined my perfect job. I believed it. When I said we'd be the size of a Pampered Chef company someday, I believed it. When I wrote the ideal qualities in a man, I believed it. When I met Gary I knew God brought him to me because I was ready for him and I had defined him in my mind and heart.

Today, I believe I will have a life of balance and inspiration. I will have time for Zach and Gary. I don't have to know how I'll do it. I just know.

Thank you, God. Thank you for a husband who understood my need to nurture myself. Thank you for giving me the strength to leave Gary and Zach and be true to my promise to me. Thank you for my financial abundance so I could revel in this incredible view and environment and enjoy this beautiful facility and sit by the fire at night and have a fabulous massage and facial. I owe You my life. I owe You to pay it forward: a life of inspiring others to understand what I now understand, as well as pay it forward to myself by having a life of focus and love and peace.

God is good. Thank you."

Each year, leaving for my personal retreat feels like the most selfish thing I can do. But I've learned that this is an investment in me. It isn't selfish. It's choosing self-love. And the resulting benefits are enormous, particularly for all the people around me.

So is this renewal time "all about me?" I don't think so. Because when Mama ain't happy, ain't *nobody* happy.

chapter four

Be Real

The Law of Realness

building trust
through humbleness.

Be Real

"If we are authentic and humble,
  we build trust in ourselves and others."

— Jill Blashack Strahan

There's a story that Alex Haley, the author of *Roots*, had a picture hanging in his office. It showed a turtle sitting on top of a fence post. Haley said he often looked at that picture to remind him of an important lesson: "If you see a turtle on a fence post, you know he had some help."

What an excellent, gentle reminder that none of us gets anywhere without the help and support of others. With every achievement and success, we need help. I admire Mr. Haley for having the picture in his office and having a visual reminder that encouraged him every day to keep things in perspective and be humble.

Alex Haley could be a poster child for Tastefully Simple's Law of Realness. Humility is at the core of this principle. When we're humble, we're not focused on ourselves and our egos. It's all about *them*. We're engaged and present. We have a mentality of serving others and knowing we're all in this together.

It's also about being kind to *ourselves.* When we trust and love ourselves we can acknowledge when we're not perfect. Then it's much easier to be honest and admit our mistakes and weaknesses. And we're also more willing to be brave and speak the truth as we see it. Humility is about saying, "Get over yourself, knock off the smoke and mirrors, and be honest."

And what is the reward for humility?

Trust. Without trust, we will build nothing of strength—our business, our marriage, the relationship with our children, our friendships, our government. When we have *trust*, all things are possible.

I've had more lessons in the Law of Realness than I care to recount, as the following stories in this section will show. But through all of these experiences I've learned and developed a keener self-awareness.

What realness is

Letting other people see who we really are

Reserving the right to get smarter

Admitting our shortcomings

Honest, straightforward conversations

Accountability for our actions

Doing the right thing

What realness is not

Smoke and mirrors

Passing the buck

Buttering it up

Being superficial

CYA (if you don't know what this is, practice the Law of Realness and ask someone!)

The Magic Moment

"Four things come not back:
the spoken word,
the spent arrow,
time past,
the neglected opportunity."

— Omar Ibn Al-Halif

When I was a teenager, Mom Scotch-taped the above quote to our avocado-green refrigerator. She'd clipped it from a magazine or newspaper and it clung there for years. I read it nearly every day.

Have you ever said something to someone that you would do *anything* to take back? As painful as it is, there's nothing we can do about it. We can't take back the spoken word. *Ever.*

At work one afternoon I was reminded about a comment I'd made to a group of people I value very much. During a conference call I had apparently remarked that they weren't working hard enough. They were upset.

I have no recollection of making the comment and I have no idea why I said it. My brains must have fallen out. I'm sure I could conjure up some excuse—I was tired that day, or frustrated about something, or what I meant to say came out wrong. The excuses don't matter. It was done and there was no way I could take back those words. The hurt was inflicted and it took time to regain their trust that I'd lost in mere seconds.

My comfort is in knowing that I'm human. I make mistakes. And the lesson learned was that I need to increase the "space in between," as Stephen Covey calls it. Or I needed to flex my "awareness muscle" and practice the "Magic Moment," as it's titled in the Pathways to Leadership training program. Both of these metaphors reference that critical space between the time something is said or happens, and the time that we respond. It's our split-second decision that will either build trust or destroy it.

When Opportunity Knocks

*"It's a good thing if your palms are a little sweaty
and you have butterflies in your stomach.
It means you're growing."*

— Jill Blashack Strahan

After graduating from Alexandria Technical College, I worked at The Marquee Too Gift Shop in Alexandria. On Sundays I would earn extra money by helping out at the Villard Café, which Dad owned.

It was a typical small town café that seated only about forty people. Dad was a farmer and knew nothing about running a restaurant, but it was important to him to keep the local café open; in a town with only 300 people it was a critical social center in the community. Of course Dad didn't have time to devote to running the café, and his absentee management was becoming a challenge.

One day Dad asked if I was interested in managing the café. He was losing money and would close the doors if I wasn't interested. I was tentative in my response because I was only twenty-one years old and had no experience in running *anything*, let alone a restaurant. But after some deliberation, I agreed. It would be a good experience for me, I wouldn't have to commute the 20 miles to work in Alexandria, and he was willing to pay me what I made at The Marquee Too. (I know. Four hundred dollars a month—pretty impressive!)

To say that my time at the Villard Café was a great experience would be an understatement. It was my introduction to entrepreneurship and my first encounter with leadership and management. I was so green I should have had leaves sprouting from my ears. To make it even more intimidating, Dad didn't just want me to manage the café. After six months, he bought the building, and put the business in my name.

It was a humbling experience to find out how much I had to learn. On my first day as the café's new manager, I walked into the kitchen and immediately spotted a brown plastic organizer attached to the stained Marlite wall. In grand disregard for the name "organizer," it was stuffed to overflowing with bills and notices. The words "Minnesota Department of Revenue" loomed large. Hmmm … ignorant as I was, I knew this was *not* a good sign.

There was a desk nestled under the staircase which served as a makeshift office, but I couldn't get close to it. Numerous brown paper bags choked the space, similarly stuffed with daily sales receipts, bank statements and other bills. When I left that night, I took everything home to my trailer house to spread out on the shag carpeting. It filled the living room. There were delinquent bills galore: sales taxes, unemployment taxes and workman's compensation withholdings. And they could have been written in Greek for all the sense they made to me.

I spent innumerable hours trying to determine the financial state of the café. The biggest lesson from those bags of paper was that if I didn't know something, tell the truth and say so. There was no way I was going to figure that mess out by myself, so I simply called the various agencies and said, "I'm new at this but I want to get you paid. What do I need to do?" Because I was upfront with them, they were very helpful and were more than willing to work with me. (And maybe all they heard was, "I want you to get paid.")

Within twelve months, I had paid off everything that was in arrears.

Telling the truth, however humbling it was, helped me in many arenas, especially with product knowledge — because I didn't have any. Heck, I didn't even like to cook, so what was I doing running a restaurant? I had to rely on my employees and my vendors to teach me the ropes.

I remember when I placed my first order with Rob, a food vendor. By the grace of God, he was the husband of Anne, a co-worker from The Marquee Too, so I knew and trusted him. It was a dark, cold November night as we sat in one of the café's wooden, high-back booths. The lighting was poor so it felt even more cold and depressing. Rob asked me what I needed. (*That* was a loaded question!)

"I know we need hamburger patties," I said.

"Four to one, six to one, or eight to one?" he said.

I said nothing, just stared blankly at him. Inside, I was thinking, "Why is he giving me odds on hamburger?"

When I said that I had no idea what he was talking about, he kindly explained the terminology as "four patties to a pound, six to a pound …" but inside I know he was thinking, "*What* is this girl doing here?"

When we ordered the canned food and he asked if I wanted the #10 can, #12 can, and so on, he didn't wait for the blank look and just explained what he meant right up front. I'm sure he thought anyone as ignorant as I was wouldn't be his customer for long, but he didn't let that stop him from trying to teach me anyway.

Probably the must humbling part of managing the café was being a leader. And I use the term loosely because I wasn't much of a leader. Nearly every one of my employees was older than I, some of them in their forties and fifties. Ruthie had owned the café when I was in high school and several of the others had worked in the restaurant business for years. What could I teach *them*? As John Maxwell said, "There goes my team. I must follow to see where I should lead them!"

I'm still thankful to them for their kindness. None of them were sarcastic, condescending or mean, and I know they must been shaking their heads as they watched this young, naive girl fumble around. But those doubts were never on display for me to see.

I operated the cafe from 1981 until 1984, and in 1982 it was renamed Jill's Grill. Running the cafe pushed me way outside my comfort zone and that was good, because we aren't learning when we're inside our comfort zone. I'll be eternally grateful to Dad for giving me such a wonderful opportunity, and to God for giving me faith to step past the fear and humility.

You Can't Give Out of an Empty Bucket

"We love others to the same degree we love ourselves.
If we don't love ourselves, we can't truly love another."

— Author Unknown

Jim and I had known each other for nearly all our lives. That was to be expected. We lived in Villard, population 300. Everyone knew everyone, and Jim's parents and my parents were friends.

I started dating Jim when I was sixteen years old and he was nineteen. He was very handsome and had a wonderful sense of humor. He was a gentleman, a good person, and a hard-working farmer. We got married five years later when I was twenty-one.

I suppose I don't need to tell you that this didn't work out. And I'm not proud. I've devoted a lot of time to scrutinizing what happened and why. To be totally honest, I was very hesitant to share my story about this. I don't want to be judged for my choices. But after much soul-searching, I've elected to share my experience with you. First, I know that there are people who will understand what I experienced. Second, this *is* a compilation of stories about realness. (Need I say more?)

Here's what I learned: choosing to leave a relationship is an enormously difficult and painful thing; the feelings of selfishness and guilt of causing someone pain never completely subsides; we love others to the same degree we love ourselves; and we have to trust ourselves and follow our heart.

Nine months after we got married, we separated. It was my idea. I was filled with unrest. I felt empty and disconnected. It wasn't Jim's fault. In retrospect, I was incapable of having an honest, self-disclosing conversation with Jim or anyone else. It was foreign to me—as well as being damn frightening. But I *wanted* to be capable of depth and meaning. I didn't want to be superficial.

We reconciled after one week. I cared deeply about Jim and I couldn't leave our marriage when I felt like I hadn't given it the time and effort it deserved.

Four months later my family did an intervention on my brother Mike, and he agreed to go to an alcoholism treatment program. Mike was twenty-three years old but he already knew that his drinking was impacting his life. As Steve used to say, "If drinking is causing a problem, you have a drinking problem."

During his one-month inpatient program, we were invited to "family week." So we all went—Mike's girlfriend, Mom, Dad, Patrick, David, David's wife and me. We attended education and counseling sessions every day for a week. Eight A.M. to nine P.M. Part of our homework was to journal every night. Theresa, our counselor, would read the journal and give us written feedback.

As you might guess, it was pretty intense. Our family dynamics were volatile. Mom and Dad had divorced a couple of years earlier so there was tension between them. We were feeling protective of Patrick, who was only eleven years old. And I was angry and frustrated much of the time. It was an emotionally charged week.

Being gently pushed and prodded and challenged by Theresa, I learned more things about myself and my life than I cared to. Theresa's first comments in my journaling notebook were, "Please chart more on your feelings." Easier said than done. I'd have to be able to *identify* a feeling!

By the end of the week, I started opening the floodgates of my heart. For the first time in my life I received permission to really look at my feelings. I didn't have to discount or rationalize them. I started to loosen up and trust myself more. Even my handwriting became less controlled and restricted as the week went on.

Jim didn't come to family week with us. He was a dairy farmer and it was difficult to take time off. I tried to share my experience with him but it was lost in translation. Family week was a turning point in my life. How could I summarize something so life-changing?

Nine months later, we separated again. These were dark days for me, and I think I'm safe in saying they were for Jim as well. He suggested we go to a pastor for marriage counseling.

I agreed. I must admit I did it halfheartedly because I wasn't sure what we would fix. I didn't know what I wanted in my life. And I certainly didn't know what a pastor could tell me that would help me feel more at peace and connected.

We saw Pastor Parks once a week for about six weeks. By the end of those six weeks he shared with us that we were both good people and that he didn't know what more he could offer.

Jim and I never reconciled. I knew I needed to figure out who I was and really understand, love and accept myself before I could give back. You can't give out of an empty bucket.

From Human Doing to Human Being

"'Come to the edge,' He said.
 They said, 'We are afraid.'

'Come to the edge,' He said.
 They came, and they flew."

    — GUILLAUME APOLLINAIRE

One Sunday morning in 1987, I was in the bathroom curling my hair when Steve answered the phone in the kitchen. I could hear him talking with Bill, a friend who was living in Sweden. After about thirty minutes he hung up and hollered to me, "Do you want to move to Sweden?"

My hand holding the curling iron stopped in mid-air. I looked back at him in the mirror as he leaned against the bathroom door frame. I could tell he was serious. Without more than a five-second pause, I said, "Yes."

My quick response still shocks me. I've always been the independent type. I don't need my hand held and I like figuring out things on my own. But I'm not particularly adventurous. If I do take a risk, it's what I would deem a calculated risk. I was twenty-eight years old and I'd traveled very little. A few years earlier my travels had been limited to driving to the Wisconsin border to go tubing down the Apple River. And I'd certainly never considered traveling to, let alone *living in*, a foreign country.

Steve and I had been married for two years. I worked at First American Bank in sales and Steve was a chemical dependency counselor, primarily working with recovering alcoholic men living at Small Beginnings, a half-way house in the upper-level apartment of our home. Alfastiftelson, a Swedish company, had several treatment centers and wanted trainers to train their counselors in the Minnesota model of treatment. If we took the opportunity, we would need to live in Sweden for nearly a year.

Without over-thinking it, I said I would go. I'd learned a lot in my job at the bank but I knew I wanted something different, something *more*. I just didn't know what that "something more" was. A hiatus in Sweden would give me time to think and ponder my next move.

So off we went to Sweden. I applied for a work visa but I didn't receive one. Oh, well. You don't need a work visa to ponder. So while Steve was busy all day training counselors and dealing with interpreters, I was in our flat, pondering.

Translation: My life came to a screeching halt. I was accustomed to being very busy and had never known anything different. What I was *doing* had always defined my life.

But now I was doing virtually nothing. I had no schedule, no meetings, no clients, no projects. Cleaning our flat took less than an hour, and that was about the only "work" I could rely on. And if I wanted to whine or complain, it was difficult to call my friends or my family. There was an eight-hour time difference, and long-distance phone calls cost money. I had to rely totally on Steve for emotional support, and Steve was busy *doing* things. I, on the other hand, had long, empty hours and I felt lost and vulnerable. Who was I if I wasn't *doing* something and wasn't being "productive"?

Fortunately we had a small circle of friends, comprising Steve's work buddies. They were wonderful, fun and interesting people. Unfortunately, my lack of identity was amplified when we were together. I felt like I was "Steve's wife" and simply an extension of him. "Jill" no longer existed.

Finally, there was the Swedish weather. It was very similar to Minnesota except we were close to the Arctic Circle—the Land of the Midnight Sun. That meant that in the winter there were approximately six hours of sunlight a day. And in 1988, those six hours were mostly gray and overcast. During January and February we had only 32 hours of sunshine. That was 1,384 hours of darkness!

I had heard that lack of light could cause depression, and now I knew it was true. I was depressed. I could feel the lifeblood running out of my body. It took effort just to move.

I found ways to take control of my downward spiral. I started working out at home three times a week and I got outdoors every day walking to the grocery store, post office and bakery. Plus I learned how to play racquetball. I was a lousy player but even so I looked forward to going into Stockholm once or twice a week to have Heidi, an eighteen-year-old American girl, whoop my butt. I also began writing a newsletter about our adventures. Every six weeks I would mail "The Scandinavian Scandal" to our friends and family back home.

All of those activities helped dramatically, and as the days became longer and the weather improved, so did my temperament. One May evening Steve and I were driving into Stockholm and I experienced something I'd never experienced before. We weren't talking about anything in particular. In fact, we were just sitting in companionable silence. And suddenly it hit me. I felt *good*. Not excited good, but serene good. Even though I wasn't doing anything, had no projects or commitments, I felt at peace. I wasn't *doing* anything. I was just *being*. And it felt right.

It was the first time in my life—all twenty-nine years of it—that I felt I was okay no matter what I did or didn't do. I was worthy of just being. After months of confusion, fear and frustration, I was no longer was a human doing. I was a human being.

Go to the Cow

*"Parties who want milk
should not seat themselves on a stool in the middle of the field
in hopes that the cow will back up to them."*

— Elbert Hubbard

I've had to learn to ask for help because it didn't come easily for me. I always thought asking for help was a sign of weakness, and I take pride in being independent. I resisted anyone's help because self-sufficiency was a measure of my strength.

Mom and Dad have assured me that even as a toddler I was headstrong and independent. My first words were "'Top it," (translation: "Stop it!") when I was being teased (tortured) by Dad and he lovingly pinched my pudgy little cheeks. And the story goes that when we were being naughty and Dad spanked us for the first time, the boys took it with stoic resolve. I bit his hand.

Not much changed over the years. Asking for help required putting my pride aside and flexing my "humility muscle." The whole thing is really quite contradictory. I have to believe I'm *worthy* of help, which means I have to have a certain amount of confidence, and at the same time I have to have the humility to be willing to ask for help. But the contradiction is an illusion. Confidence and humility go together; they're complements, not opposites. We have to have high self-esteem in order to admit our weaknesses.

Another reason we might not ask for help is because we're being a martyr. And I hate to admit this, but sometimes I can be a martyr. Saying, "I can do it all myself" can be a cowardly way of saying, "Poor, poor pitiful me. Look at my sorry lot in life. I *have* to do this all myself." I can bask in the glow of their sympathy or attention or whatever. I can play the victim.

Last, I avoid asking for help because I don't want to "bother" anyone. What's fascinating to me about that notion is that when other people ask *me* for help, I don't consider it a bother. Usually I feel flattered, and I want to help them out. When I ask someone to help me, it gives us an opportunity to build a stronger relationship.

Knowing that I need help at times does not mean that I'm incompetent or stupid or any of those other negative labels I used to hang on myself. In fact, just the opposite. The ability to recognize our needs and act appropriately *defines* competence and intelligence. When I first started Tastefully Simple, my knee-jerk response was that it was more efficient for me to do things by myself than to ask someone to help me. It took some time and a lot of energy for me to realize I was squandering my valuable time by not using all the available resources. *Not* a smart or competent way to run a company!

The Law of Realness has taught me that I was wrong. Now I go to the cow when I need milk.

Graham Crackers

"Courage is not the absence of fear,
but rather the judgment that something else is more important than fear."

∽— AMBROSE REDMOON

I'd been holed up in my home office for the entire day, continuing to run numbers and re-run numbers for Tastefully Simple's first five-year business plan. How many consultants would we have each year? How many parties would they be doing? What would their average party sales be?

Creative Memories had been a huge gift to us. They sell scrapbooks and accessories for preserving photos and memorabilia through direct sales and home classes. In January 1995 the co-founders, Cheryl Lightle and Rhonda Anderson, along with several key people from their team, met with Joani and me. We ran the concept by them and had them taste-test several of the products. They gave us their gut reactions to our ideas and shared what they'd learned in the business. They were a wonderful role model for me in their attitude of abundance.

They also shared their impressive numbers. By the end of 1994 they had 3,600 consultants, and had achieved $9 million dollars in sales. When we heard this, our adrenalin was pumping.

What excited us most was that they were selling a somewhat consumable product, but we were going to be selling *food*. We'd only sell to people who eat! So we had the distinct advantage of repeat sales. Once someone taste-tested Bountiful Beer Bread or Spinach and Herb Mix, they'd be hooked because the products were superb.

I can't tell you how many times I ran various calculations over the next few weeks. How would I know how many consultants I'd have or how many parties they'd do or how many people would attend the party or how much they'd spend at each party? It felt like a crapshoot. But eventually I landed on a scenario that felt right and doable. And suddenly the adrenalin pumping through my blood turned to ice. My projections showed *eleven million dollars* in sales at the end of five years.

I was stunned. I slowly got up from my desk, walked down the hall to the kitchen in a daze, opened the cupboard and reached for a box of graham crackers. Then I got out the Land O' Lakes butter and a knife and standing in the corner between the stove and the refrigerator, I proceeded to shove buttered graham crackers, one after another, into my mouth. (Come on. Don't *you* eat when you're stressed?)

Eleven million dollars. That's a lot of money. I picked up the phone to call Joani. I knew she'd be working at Salon Alexis, because she was a working fiend, and I knew she'd probably be with a client, but I called her anyway. Miraculously, she answered the phone.

"Joani. I've finally landed on some pretty sound projections. I'm showing that this is going to be an eleven-million-dollar company in five years. Joani. I can't *run* an eleven-million-dollar company."

There was a poetic pause on the other end of the phone and then I heard these wise words.

"Jill, if you can *grow* an eleven-million-dollar company, you can *run* an eleven-million-dollar company."

As I absorbed her words, I heard myself saying, "You know Joani, you're right. I don't entirely agree, but I suppose once we're an eleven-million-dollar company we could afford to *hire* someone to run the company."

I can always count on Joani for a fresh perspective. She was such a blessing to me and her words were exactly what I needed to hear. She reassured me when fear started to erode my belief. It's so very important that we have people like Joani around us, people who look for what's right with the world, people who dream big.

And equally important, we have to be willing to reach out to those incredible people, be honest about our fears, trust them and ask for what we need.

Rejection Hangover

"I wanted a perfect ending.
Now I've learned, the hard way, that some poems don't rhyme
and some stories don't have a clear beginning, middle and end.
Life is about not knowing, having to change,
taking the moment and making the best of it,
without knowing what's going to happen next.
Delicious ambiguity."

— GILDA RADNER IN *IT'S ALWAYS SOMETHING*

Business plan? Done! Start-up money? Done! Marketing materials? Done! Inventory ordered? Done! Parties booked? Oops!

Having parties booked and on the calendar is the lifeblood of a home party business. I had no idea how to make booking calls, but I liked people and knew they'd love our taste-testing party. I started by going through a list of people who had told me they'd like to have a party once I got the business up and running. I had twenty people on the list and I figured it would take me at least an hour to call them all. It was important that I get my parties booked within the next couple of months. I didn't want people to wait until September or October. I needed those party bookings now. Without the parties, there was no Tastefully Simple.

So on a beautiful June evening while Zach and Steve were playing in the back yard, I sat down at my desk in my makeshift office in front of the telephone.

Two hours later I had called every person on my list. I left a bunch of messages on a bunch of answering machines and the few people that I actually managed to reach told me they wanted to have a party but not within the next two months.

By the end of the evening, I had only one party booked. I was discouraged and fearful. How was this going to work if I couldn't even get a booking from people who *wanted* to have a party?

The next morning I went to the office (aka The Shed) still bummed out from the "rejections" of the night before. I was taking it personally and was suffering from a rejection hangover.

Within an hour, the phone rang. It was Kelly Detterding from Spectrum Printing. Kelly and her husband, Roger, owned Spectrum and they were printing the catalog. My first thought was, "Oh no. I have to have my catalogs by my first party. Please don't tell me they aren't going to be ready!"

Instead, I heard Kelly say, "I'm looking at your catalog and I was just wondering what Tastefully Simple is. Are you a home party company?" (Oops! I guess I didn't do a very good job writing the marketing copy if she had to ask.)

I explained that it was and she said, "This sounds really cool. I'd like to book a party."

After getting her party scheduled for July 2, I hung up, leaned back in my chair, looked up at the ceiling with my arms outstretched and said out loud, "*Thank you, Lord*!" I paused for a second, and then said, "Just send me one of those calls every day and everything will be just fine!"

It was a humbling experience when I wasn't getting what I wanted. That one call renewed me. Because of Kelly, I believed again. I ended up having six parties between June 15 and July 15. Those bookings spawned more bookings, and from there things started to rock and roll. In November I had eighteen parties.

Eventually, nearly all of the original people on my list booked a party. They just hadn't done it according to *my* time schedule.

Swallow

"You stumble only if you're moving."

⌒ Roberto Goizuete
a former CEO, Coca-Cola

I did my first party on June 15, 1995. On July 2, I did Kelly Detterding's party in Little Falls, Minnesota, one hour north of Alexandria. It was a great party. She had over $500 in sales plus several bookings for other parties. I was pumped.

As I was packing up, the telephone rang. Kelly handed it to me, saying that it was Tanya, one of the guests who'd just left the party. A bit perplexed, I answered the phone.

"Hi, Jill. This is Tanya. Would it be possible for you to stop by my house on your way out of town? I'm interested in selling Tastefully Simple products and I'd like to have you talk with my husband, John, and me."

I was shell-shocked. Several people had expressed interest in the business during my first few parties but no one had requested a one-to-one meeting with me the same night as a party! I hesitantly explained that I'd love to come over but I didn't have any written information or formal presentation. Tanya didn't care and asked if I'd come anyway. (Golly gee whiz. Let me think about that. Okay!) It was nearly 10:30 at night when I got to their home. We sat in their three-season porch and I began my stellar sales pitch by walking them through the twelve-page compensation plan.

Duh! I was pathetic. I didn't ask Tanya what got her excited about what she'd seen at the party. I didn't ask questions to find out what she wanted from the business. Was it flexibility or money or friendships or to be home more or to get a life?

And who on earth creates a twelve-page compensation plan and uses that to share all the benefits? Tanya later told me that she mentally glazed over and didn't hear a word I said.

Number One Tanya Lesson: Keep it simple. In spite of my salesmanship, or lack thereof, Tanya signed up to become a consultant. But needless to say, within a short time I created a one-page compensation summary!

The second lesson was more humbling. There had been approximately five people at Kelly's party who indicated they were interested in having a party, all of whom were in the Little Falls area. I'm embarrassed to admit that I never considered giving those parties to Tanya.

Fortunately, Tanya was brave. She called me and said that she would like my bookings. After all, she said, she lived in Little Falls, and if I came up from Alexandria I would in essence be doing parties for her future clients, which didn't make a lot of sense.

After hearing her out, I told her I'd think about it and get back to her. I hung up feeling irritated, defensive and territorial. It didn't feel right to give her the parties. I continued to struggle with my emotions over the next 24 hours as I processed her feedback.

By the next day I decided Tanya was right. I needed the income from those parties but I concluded that the short-term gain wouldn't outweigh the long-term gain of helping Tanya build her clientele. And my clients would be better served by having a local consultant.

I swallowed hard and called her. I admitted I was wrong and that she should have my bookings from Kelly's party. And to this day I recommend that consultants "gift" their bookings when it's geographically logical for another consultant to service those clients or when their calendar is too full.

Number Two Tanya Lesson: Take a dose of humility, swallow hard and admit when I'm wrong. I'd been short-sighted and was holding on too tightly. In retrospect, it was a pivotal point for me. Not only was I slapped with the Law of Realness, I was pushed around by the Law of Abundancy through my selfishness and my focus on scarcity. I wasn't looking at the big picture and win-win solutions.

It didn't end there though. After that experience, I thought it was a win-win decision to "gift" my new consultants to other sponsors, even though I recruited them. My intention was to help consultants build their business and their confidence.

Unfortunately, it backfired on me. First, I violated the value of earning their team. Sure, they became Team Leaders more quickly, but they hadn't earned it. I gave it to them. The psychological impact of that was huge. Down deep they knew it wasn't their team. It was mine. And the long-term effect was that it reduced their self-confidence. Second, it created a strong reliance on me for leading their team and they didn't develop their leadership skills. And third, they began to expect that I would continue gifting new consultants to them and consequently didn't build their skills in sharing the opportunity.

We all learn as we go along. We will not know it all when we dive into something new and different. We'll make mistakes — but that's when we simply swallow our pride, admit our mistakes, learn from the experience and move on.

We Never Fail

"We don't know what we don't know."

— Author Unknown

Scientists at NASA built a gun specifically to launch dead chickens at the windshields of airliners, military jets and the space shuttles, all traveling at maximum velocity. The idea was to simulate collisions with airborne fowl, to test the strength of the windshields.

British engineers heard about the gun and were eager to test it on the windshields of their high-speed trains. Arrangements were made and a gun was sent to the British engineers. When the gun was fired, the engineers stood shocked as the chicken hurled out of the barrel, crashed through the shatterproof shield smashing it to smithereens, blasted through the control console, snapped the engineer's backrest in two and embedded itself in the back wall of the cabin.

The horrified Brits sent NASA the results of the disastrous experiment, along with the designs of the windshield and begged the US scientists for suggestions.

NASA responded with a one-line memo.

"Defrost the chicken."

I love that story. And I admire the Brits in this story. They embraced the Law of Realness. As soon as their windshield shattered, they were on the phone asking for help.

There have been plenty of times in my life where I've metaphorically thrown frozen chickens at windshields—and broken a lot of windshields! But many years ago I took the word "failure" out of my vocabulary. Today I only have "lessons learned."

Again, life is not a straight line. It's really quite *curly*. We rarely know exactly how we're going to get where we're going or what to expect when we get there. We just dive in and do it. If it doesn't work, we learn from it.

Admitting that we make mistakes does not mean that we're a failure. It just means that we might have to defrost a chicken or two next time.

We Reserve the Right to Get Smarter

"If we were supposed to be perfect,
spell check wouldn't have been created."

— AUTHOR UNKNOWN

We reserve the right to get smarter. I can't tell you how many times this adage has saved me.

In the beginning years of Tastefully Simple I had no preconceived notion of how things should be done—and frankly, I had absolutely no *clue* what I was doing. Without experience in the home party industry (other than doing two or three parties as a Rubbermaid consultant at the age of nineteen) and having been self-taught through the school of hard knocks, I reserved the right to get smarter countless times.

What I didn't have in experience and product knowledge, I made up for in enthusiasm. For the first few months at my parties, I would proudly hold up the jar of Honey Mustard, and because I cooked very little and had minimal experience with the product I would say, "This is our Honey Mustard. I *love* this on sandwiches." I would then caution them that there was a little kick to the mustard and they'd experience the "bite" of horseradish.

And then I'd pass it around for the guests to taste-test on pretzels.

One evening I was totaling the guests' orders at the end of the party. One of the guests was standing in line, clearly wanting to ask a question. She was holding a jar of Honey Mustard.

I felt something coming. The Law of Realness started to circle around and around above my head, ready to swoop down on me.

Sure enough. She said, "I really love this Honey Mustard, but I don't see that it contains horseradish."

OMG. (Translation: Oh, my *God!*)

I looked up at her, my eyes wide. "Really?"

I quickly took the jar from her hands, suspiciously turning it over to scrutinize the ingredients. Time stood still as I read the ingredients. And re-read them.

"Oh my gosh, you're *right*. There *isn't* any horseradish in here!"

And then I exclaimed with great enthusiasm, "It sure *tastes* like it has horseradish, doesn't it?!" She agreed.

And that was the end of it. I didn't beat myself up. I didn't fall all over myself apologizing. I didn't feel ashamed. (Well, maybe a little.) It was a genuine error on my part. Because wouldn't you agree that if it *tastes* like horseradish it must *be* horseradish?

I've learned that when I reserve the right to get smarter, it lets me be authentic as well as freeing me from having to be perfect. Goodness knows there's nothing quite as humbling as admitting when we're wrong. Mistakes are as much a part of the process of our growth as doing things "right." One of the great things about being real is that we give ourselves permission to stumble. As long as we can be honest, not get bogged down and learn how to move on, there's always an opportunity to grow. I relied heavily on our consultants, our clients and our own intuition to help us figure things out as we went along.

As it turned out my "strategy" was the recipe for three main dishes: a ton of mistakes, the opportunity to be real, and to have some amazing discoveries. I could have waited to have my first few parties until I'd studied up on all the ingredients in our products. And I could have waited until I'd perfected my script. And I could have waited to have the ideal catalog. And I could have waited until … you get the joke.

But if we're fearful and we wait until everything is perfect and the conditions are "just right," we're more than likely going to sit on the sidelines and watch while someone else makes things happen. Sometimes we have to just dive in and do it, reserving the right to get smarter.

Feeling Gritchy

"Babe Paley, a socialite and an accomplished hostess,
set standards of excellence so high that no one could begin to rival her good taste.
A keen observer of social blunders, Truman Capote wrote,
'Mrs. P. had only one fault.
She was perfect; otherwise, she was perfect.'"

— VERONIQUE VIENNE IN *THE ART OF IMPERFECTION*

Here's an open secret: I'm not always that Gung Ho.

I don't always have an upbeat, positive attitude. I'm not the kind of person who jumps out of bed in the morning raring to go. I've been known to hit the snooze button more than once. And some days I bet other people who have to be around me wish I had hit it again. And again. There are simply days when I'm not overly motivated or when I'm "intense." In fact, there are days when I'm grouchy and, well ... gritchy.

When I'm feeling uptight or irritated about something, I try to put things in perspective. I ask myself, "How important is this, *really*? In a hundred years, when I'm dead and gone and just worm meat, is this going to matter?"

Sometimes putting it in perspective helps. Sometimes it doesn't. Sometimes all the profound, well-meant self-talk in the world won't chase the gritchiness away. Those are the times I just have to do something to get rid of it.

I can still recall one morning shortly after we'd moved Tastefully Simple to our second location on Nokomis Street. Steve had died in August and two weeks later we left our beloved shed. Life had been a little crazy. On this particular morning I felt edgy and unsettled when I came into work. I'm sure everyone sensed it as I forced out a constipated "Good morning" and stalked past them to go into my office. I worked at my desk for a few moments, trying to shake off the clinging gritchiness.

I was unsuccessful. Finally I got up, walked out of my office, stood in the doorway, put my hands on my hips, and announced: "All right. I'm PMS'ing and I'm in a *really* bad mood! Just wanted you to know!"

I paused for a second and then said, "Okay. I feel better now." As I turned and walked back into my office, everyone started to laugh, including me. It felt like one hundred pounds were lifted from me.

I wasn't telling them anything they didn't know already. People always know when we're in a bad mood, even when we try to hide it. There is something very powerful in being upfront and honest, telling it like it is. The act of simply acknowledging the elephant in the living room is significant. The negative energy no longer has power. *We* do. By stating how I felt, I expended some of that negativity and started the energy moving in a positive direction.

Since that time, Jane Nachbor, our Marketing Director, came up with a great idea to get the energy moving again in her team. If they're feeling overwhelmed and frustrated they execute a primal scream. They step outside the building onto the lawn, share a thirty-second explanation of the source of their frustration and, as a group, everyone *screams* at the top of their lungs.

Law of Realness? Absolutely! And I bet they come away feeling purged and renewed.

Dusty Soaps

"There's more than one right answer."

— Dewitt Jones

I've said it before and I'll say it again. Life is full of contradictions. It's never linear.

When my friend Sue was a child, her mom had an oversized glass jar filled with little soaps in her bathroom. You know the kind I'm talking about—delicate, pretty, colorful soaps that are to be admired but never used. During the 1960s this was a very "in" decorating trend.

Sue was not allowed to use these precious soaps, and over time the little soaps started to fade and become dusty. In spite of their lackluster appearance, the jar of dusty soaps became shrine-like and sat on the vanity for years.

Eventually, her mom decided to redecorate the bathroom and, as they were packing up everything to begin the project, Sue was shocked to see her mom pick up the soap jar, turn it upside down and unceremoniously dump all of the soaps into the garbage! Sue was incredulous. Weren't these soaps a treasure? These precious, delicate, pretty, colorful soaps suddenly were just *garbage*? What was her mother thinking?

Seeing her daughter's expression, her mom shrugged and said, "What? It's just a bunch of dusty old soap!"

For Sue's mom, as she created the vision for her new bathroom and redefined what she wanted to achieve, saw them as "a bunch of dusty old soap" and chose to dispose of them. Indeed, she hadn't really seen those soaps for years. When people take things for granted, they cease to see or value them. However, others may see value. For Sue, the untouchable soaps represented something sacred. It took a radical shift in her perspective for her to see them as garbage.

I've had dusty soaps in my life, those ideas that I cling to because I perceive them as sacred. I used to "know" that our Tastefully Simple products sold very well with an illustrated catalog. I "knew" that all Tastefully Simple consultants had to have inventory at their parties because clients wanted to walk out the door with their purchase. I used to "know" that you had to sample nearly every product at a party in order to have great sales.

And then someone said or did something that helped me see that there are new and better ways. Now we have a full-color catalog with gorgeous photography. Our consultants are inventory-free and we ship direct to every client's door. We reduced the sampling at parties to fifteen to twenty items so our guests weren't stuffed to the gills.

Ploop! I threw my dusty soaps in the garbage and redefined my reality.

I've learned the importance of always looking for more than one right answer. I always need to be on the lookout for dusty soaps, those little things that are so easy to overlook and grow accustomed to, even though they may be stale, boring and, well, dusty.

Performance Review

"If 'ifs and buts' were candy and nuts,
we'd all have a Merry Christmas!"

ⅎ— Don Meredith

Like most companies, we do annual performance reviews at Tastefully Simple headquarters. We call them "Success Reviews" and part of our process includes having your peers evaluate you.

Well, I hadn't had a peer review in a couple of years, so in September 2001 I decided it was high time I did. Using the same process we use for all of our HQ team, I had the people on my team evaluate me. They used thirty-seven questions in five categories that we used for everyone: team player, attitude, competency and organization, leadership, and communication.

The survey was anonymous and they ranked my performance on a scale of 1 to 6, with 6 being outstanding. The questions were things like *shares credit and recognition for a job well done*, or *is easy to approach with a problem or concern*, or *is punctual* or *takes initiative to get things done*.

Friday evening, after a long day of continuous meetings, I walked into my office at 5:45 feeling very stressed. And lucky me! The final tabulations from my peer review were in a large sealed manila envelope on my chair.

I opened the envelope, skimming through the results. Ever so slowly I slid the evaluation back into the envelope and walked out of my office.

The results were horrible! All the way home I rolled them over and over in my mind. As I walked into the house, the tears that had been threatening to overflow began to stream down my face.

I felt totally deflated. The only way I could correct my weaknesses was to work more hours. But I knew that wasn't realistic. I couldn't give any more of myself. I was working 80 hours a week and didn't give Zach the time he deserved. I gave everything humanly possible to the business.

My lowest average score, on a scale of 1 to 6, was a 3.5 on my *ability to organize and prepare in a way that reduces having to work in a crisis mode.* I had an average of 3.6 on how *easy I am to approach with a problem or concern* and an average of 3.8 on *punctuality*. I kept seeing those numbers in my mind… 3.8 … 3.6 … 3.5. Such a very long way from 6.0!

"Well, how can I prepare if I don't close my door? And if I close my door, how can I be approachable? And if I didn't have so many blasted meetings, I could be more punctual." Yada, yada, yada.

Wahhhh. Poor me.

The bottom line was that the evaluations were right, and I knew it. Actually I knew that my team was probably being *kind* in some areas. They could easily have scored me even lower.

And keep in mind it was *my* perception that my evaluation was terrible. I wanted all As. But I ignored the As and focused only on the Bs and Cs.

Finally I thought, "Knock it off, Jill, and get over it! There are no surprises here. Just figure out ways to work on your challenge areas, starting with ways to compact your time and delegate more so you can be fully present to others."

Was this a painful and humbling experience? Absolutely! But you know what? It forced me to suck it up, look at my shortcomings and work on becoming a better leader. Today, my goal is to have a minimum overall average score of 5.4. And I've achieved that every year since 2003.

Worthy of Good

"Like wealth itself, opportunity is not a matter of things or events,
it is an attitude, a way of seeing the world.
Opportunity is saying,
'No matter what happens to me,
I will use it for my upliftment, learning and growth.'"

— AUTHOR UNKNOWN

Receiving the Ernst & Young Entrepreneur of the Year award was a huge honor. Oddly, receiving the award also made me feel very, very humble. I struggled with my feelings.

Choking back my tears, I admitted to Elizabeth, my counselor, that I felt unworthy of winning the award. "There's no one I can talk to about these feelings," I said. "I'm afraid they'll think I'm being ungrateful and unappreciative. Don't get me wrong, Elizabeth. I loved getting the recognition and the award. I'm just overwhelmed by these feelings of unworthiness. I didn't deserve it. There were so many other people and companies that were more deserving than me. Why did I win? I was no more special than any other CEO in the room. Sure, I worked hard, but a *lot* of people have worked hard building their business and they weren't on that stage. Plus, there were so many factors involved in Tastefully Simple's success … the grace of God, the sacrifices that Dolly and Joey made, the belief that Joani had."

Elizabeth then asked me a mind-boggling question. "Jill, do you believe you've deserved the *bad* things that happened to you in your life? Did you deserve to have your brothers die or to have Steve die? Why don't you deserve to have *good* things happen to you, too?"

The impact of Elizabeth's words hit me hard. I knew that I *hadn't* deserved the bad things in my life. They could have just as easily happened to someone else. There was a reason they had happened to me. I had something to learn from the pain. So why couldn't I simply accept this recognition as a good thing that I "deserved" as much as I "deserved" the bad things that had happened?

She was right. What made this any different?

Thanks to Elizabeth's words, I felt *clean*. I no longer felt like a fraud. I realized that God has blessed me with all I've learned through challenges and pain. And he's graced me with *huge* blessings in my life, like Tastefully Simple and the Ernst & Young award.

Who am I to think that I can choose what's given to me?

chapter five

Burning Bright

Burning Bright

"It doesn't interest me what you do for a living.
I want to know what you ache for
and if you dare to dream of meeting your heart's longing.

It doesn't interest me how old you are.
I want to know if you will risk looking like a fool for love,
for your dream,
for the adventure of being alive."

— ORIAH MOUNTAIN DREAMER
in *OPENING THE INVITATION*

Everything and anything starts with a dream.

I know what some of you are thinking. "Dreaming doesn't produce results. It's pie in the sky and Pollyanna-ish."

Well, I believe you're already a dreamer. You may not realize it consciously, but at some level we *all* have hopes and dreams. You have some small dreams, and you may be harboring some BHAGs – Big, Hairy, Audacious Goals, as Jim Collins refers to them.

Just the word "dream" itself is powerful. I'm inspired whenever I hear a recording of Martin Luther King saying, "I have a dream." Perhaps because I relate to Webster's dictionary definition of a dream: "a cherished aspiration, ambition or ideal." I love that definition: cherished aspirations, ambitions or ideals.

Yet when we call someone a dreamer, it's usually negative and connotes someone who's out of touch. And to be fair, I need to tell you that the dictionary also defines a dream as "an unrealistic or self-deluding fantasy."

Ouch!

But I have to acknowledge it because this is *exactly* where the rubber meets the road; this negative overtone is where we get all hung up about daring to dream. Because how do we really *know* when a dream is truly an aspiration, ambition or ideal? How can we tell if our dreams turn an unpleasant corner and become "unrealistic, self-deluding fantasies"? What defines the difference between an aspiration and a delusional fantasy?

Here's what I've learned: that's up to us. We're in control of our own lives.

So, picture it. You have a dream, an ideal, something that you could really see yourself working toward and becoming passionate about. You've set your bar high — to a place that excites you.

Then your dad, or a teacher, or your Great-Aunt Sally, or some other dream stealer, tells you that you're being unrealistic. You can't do that, they say. You're dreaming. It will never happen.

And you buy into it. I can hear that big old sucking sound. With warp speed you're sucked into their sewer of negativity. You hear that nasty old Scarcity Voice and within mere seconds, you yank your bar back down to meet *their* low expectations of life.

When we hear these things from people we care about — that our dreams are unrealistic, self-deluding fantasies — we convince ourselves that they're right. We listen to the naysayers and we stop believing. We throw away our dream, our cherished aspiration, our ideal. It lays there untouched. We chicken out. We allow ourselves to believe we can't have it. We're being ridiculous. What was I thinking? They're right. I'm not worthy of it.

Right?

Wrong!

You are worthy of your dreams. You can have the life you deserve.

In this book I've shared some of my dreams with you. I didn't just dream, of course. I also *believed* in my dreams. And I was willing to *work* to make them happen. I now know that if you can see it, you can have it.

I learned that if I don't believe in my dreams with all my heart and work toward them with undying effort, I don't have a dream. I just have a thought. A wimpy, wispy thought. A *gosh-wouldn't-it-be-nice-if* idea.

Those types of thoughts, those *gosh-wouldn't-it-be-nice-if* thoughts are *not* dreams. Perhaps they are the precursors to a dream, but they are not a cherished dream that we truly believe in, deep down in our heart.

And believing in ourselves doesn't happen overnight. It doesn't just appear one day because we want it to. Developing that belief in ourselves is part of a journey. It's developed day-by-day, experience after experience.

If we want to keep our dreams alive, we must be intentional about it. Otherwise they'll fade and start to feel like delusional fantasies. So what can we do to stay motivated? When things get difficult, how do we continue to dream and believe? There are five primary ways that I've learned to renew my dreams and my belief:

Expect adversity

Life isn't perfect. There may be big, gut-wrenching punches of adversity, and I will guarantee you there will be little, irritating pinches along the way. Like when people would say, in their condescending sing-song voice, "So, how's your little business doing?"

And I would smile and nod and say, "Fine, thank you." And my heart would be aching to say, "You just wait. Someday you'll see."

Adversity as well as anger can be excellent motivators. Use the energy positively and smile and nod.

Surround yourself with positive influences

Hang out with people who believe in you: family, friends or mentors who can help you hold onto your dreams and remind you of what you want your ideal life to be. We need them to encourage us to pursue those ideals, helping us to overcome the naysayers and the dream stealers.

And you never know when they'll give you little unexpected boosts. I still remember things that Glennie did. When I was twenty-five years old she was my supervisor at First American Bank. She'd read a magazine article about characteristics of successful people, one of which was "successful people typically walk fast." She looked me square in the eye and said, "*You* walk fast."

What I heard Glennie say was, "You're going to be successful."

After all these years, I vividly remember her words. I was blessed to have many people like Glennie around me who believed in me and influenced my life in countless ways.

Set goals

Set goals, my friends!

Many of us often attribute success to people's character or style: their energy or cheerful disposition or down-to-business nature. This translates to "I can't be successful because I'm not like Jane." I've seen Tastefully Simple consultants who are bouncing off the walls with enthusiasm succeed. I've seen that same style fail. I've seen consultants who are serious and steady as a rock succeed. I've seen that same style fail.

The characteristic that successful consultants *do* have in common is that they have serious thoughts about their life and their Tastefully Simple business. They build their business with intent. And they set goals and they write them down.

I can't say it often enough: *Goal setting works.* Write them down, or have a Discovery Journal. Revisit them on a regular basis. They will help you re-ignite your dream and begin to believe again. And remember, if a goal doesn't come to fruition, then it wasn't for your ultimate good.

Help others move toward their dreams

That's right. Get out of yourself and help someone else.

I'll often hear from successful people that they've reached a point in their lives where they need to find ways to motivate themselves again. I totally understand. Tell me this: Is it possible to talk to someone who's fresh and eager and passionate about their hopes and dreams and not be totally energized when we walk away? Their energy rubs off on us and we become more excited about our own possibilities. It helps remind us to get back to dreaming and doing what gets us excited.

Consistently work it

What transforms dreaming and believing into success is the willingness to make it happen through *action*. Yet the only way we're going to be willing to consistently work it is if the first two foundations, dreaming and believing, are aligned. If we don't believe in ourselves, no matter how hard we work, we won't bring our dreams to fruition. Something will continue to get in the way.

For many of us, dreaming and believing seem nebulous, like nailing Jell-O to a tree. Dreaming is in our heads; believing is in our hearts. But working it? That brings it all down to our hands. There's a reference to Michelangelo's work that I've loved for years: "He saw an angel in the stone and carved to set it free." He saw it in his head, he believed it in his heart, and he made it a reality by using tools to carve it out of stone.

Like Michelangelo, when we persist and work hard, we witness an evolution. One-by-one-by-one, one chink at a time, we see progress. We can only grow one inch at a time. We can only lose weight one pound at a time. We can only save money one dollar at a time. We can only build a house one brick or board at a time. We can only build a loving relationship one conversation at a time, one action at a time.

We all know that nothing happens overnight. It's persisting and actually doing the work, even when we sometimes don't feel like it. I know how easy it is to come up with excuses. But excuses are like arm pits: everyone has a couple of them up their sleeves and they all *stink*.

When all else fails

And last but not least: when all else fails, *fake it 'til you make it*.

chapter six

Choose to Shine

Choose to Shine

"There are some souls on this earth that just seem to shine a little brighter.
It's not because they've been left to burn in peace and quiet.
I think it's because they've been stirred—and poked and prodded.
The fire grows and glows because of the beautiful struggle they're in.
The flame gets a little hotter,
The heart a little stronger,
And the soul so very, very bright.
You shine."

— JODI HILLS

During the past couple of weeks as I was completing this book, I've spent more time at home than I have in the past ten years. I've been in the sitting room with my laptop on my lap (why they call it a laptop) and my feet up on the rattan ottoman, complete with my fuzzy black socks. I've been able to think and create and contemplate and tweak while I've looked out over the snow and trees and frozen lake. I've had the music playing, and most importantly, I've had a fire in the fireplace.

I love a fire in the fireplace. No doubt because Mom would start a fire on Christmas Eve or when there was a snowstorm or when she was simply moved to do so. And the whole mood of our home would change: I felt more relaxed and open and centered. I love a fire in the fireplace.

On the other hand, a fire can be really, really annoying, especially when you're trying to write a book. I would get up and add more firewood. I'd go out to the garage several times a day to get more wood. If the wood was too hard or too soft the fire burned too slow or too fast. As it started to die, I'd stir it and poke it and prod it. And then it would ignite itself and I would sit back, with a sense of satisfaction and gratitude for the victory.

Then it would start all over again. I finally concluded that there's a reason why women stayed home in the old days to "stoke the home fires." It occupied their entire day! Stirring and poking and prodding. Mama mia! (And I'm not even Italian.)

But you know, every single time I engaged in this ritual, I thought of Jodi Hills' quote. Every single time, without fail.

Because every single time, without fail, I would think of life being this way. I'd think of all the wise and wonderful people I know, whom I honor and respect, who've been stirred and poked and prodded in life. And I've witnessed their flame, and their heart, and their soul.

And they do shine so very, very bright — because they *choose* to shine. They haven't been left to burn quietly, or worse yet, let their flame die.

Life isn't always perfect, my friend. But it is overflowing with teachings. These teachings aren't meant to hurt us or deter us. They're meant to stir and poke and prod us, so we live our lives more fully, with more meaning, and more intent. These teachings are there to help us simply shine.

With Deep Gratitude

These pages have been the most difficult to write. It's not that I find it difficult to thank people — my heart is brimming over with love and appreciation for the countless blessings God has given me. (And He's the first to be thanked!) My concern is how can I begin to thank all the people who've contributed to this book? There are over 60 stories in *Simply Shine* and nearly every one is about people who've impacted my life. So to all of you referenced in these pages, *thank you*! I'm a better person because of you.

As a CEO, the network created through my Vistage group has been priceless. Walt Sutton, thank you for your abundant and giving nature. As the author of *Leap of Strength* you shared your pearls of wisdom and knowledge, including the resource of Jan King. Jan is the founder and editorial director of eWomenPublishingNetwork. If any of you are considering writing a book, she's your woman! And to Susan Scott I also send my deep appreciation. You've helped me in my journey in many ways, one of which being your experience in writing *Fierce Conversations*.

Kim Pearson, my amazing editor, you had an uncanny ability to crawl into my head — and come back out alive! To Dawn Putney and the team at Toolbox Creative, my gratitude for your guidance and creativity in cover design and page layout, as well as connecting us with our copy editor, proofreader and printer, Thomson-Shore.

In true Tastefully Simple fashion, the headquarters team has lived up to their reputation for teamwork, dedication and exceeding expectations. Jennifer Panchenko, VP of Marketing; Jane Nachbor, Marketing Director; Lynn Grueneich, Communications Senior Lead; Matt Jensen, Design Crew Senior Lead; as well as, Carmen Johnson, Marketing Manager and Terri Ellman, Public Relations Coordinator — your leadership has made this dream come true. *You all simply shine!*

Others who have been unyielding in their quest for excellence are Jen Thompson, Juliet Ray, Angie Peschl, Tresa Schmidt—and my dear friend, Sue Weber, who always gives me gentle yet forthright feedback.

Joani Nielson, your relentless commitment to making Tastefully Simple the best it can be is unsurpassed. Although you're laser focused, you make time to let your spiritedness shine through. It's a blessing working with you!

On a personal note, to my heavenly angels: Thank you, Dad. Although I know you're always with me, I wish with all my heart I could share this with you in this world. And Mike, Pat and Steve—thank you for enriching my life and helping me understand the importance of living *today.*

To my earthly angels: Mom, if you ever had doubts you never showed it. You believed in me, stood by me, and taught me priceless lessons in life. To my brother David, thank you for modeling 'one day at a time' and for making the best of what you're given. To my son Zach, I'm grateful for your honesty, patience and love. You have always been my greatest blessing. To my Beautiful Man, Gary Strahan, what words are there? I can't imagine anyone who could be more loving and kind and generous and genuinely supportive than you. Not only are you a magnificent husband, but such a good father to Zach that my heart melts every time I see you together.

And last but not least, to the thousands of Tastefully Simple consultants across the nation, I say again: my heart brims over with love and appreciation—and pride. You have impacted countless lives in countless ways. This book would not be possible without your dreams, your belief and your hard work. You persevere and you choose to shine.

For Their Abundant Hearts

I would also like to gratefully acknowledge all of the writers and leaders quoted in this book for their inspiration, passion and wisdom. We conducted an extensive search to determine whether previously published quotations in this book required permission to reprint. If any errors have occurred, however, please accept my sincere apologies—and rest assured, a correction will be made in future editions.

The following authors, agents, and publishers have graciously granted permission to include excerpts from the following:

Fish! Video © Charthouse International Learning Corporation. Used with permission from Charthouse International.

Maxwell, Dr. John C. All of Dr. Maxwell's leadership resources are available at maximumimpact.com. Used by permission from Dr. John C. Maxwell.

Oriah Mountain Dreamer. (1994). *Opening the Invitation*. Harper San Francisco. Reprinted by permission of Harper Collins Publishers, Inc.

Overton, Patrick. (1975). *The Leaning Tree*. Bethany Press. Reprinted by permission from Patrick Overton.

Overton, Patrick. (1997). *Rebuilding the Front Porch of America*. Columbia College. Reprinted by permission from Patrick Overton.

Radner, Gilda. (1989). *It's Always Something*. Simon & Schuster. Reprinted by permission from Michael Radner.

Vienne, Veronique. (1999). *The Art of Imperfection*. New York: Clarkson N. Potter Publishers. Reprinted by permission of Clarkson Potter Publishers.

Williamson, Marianne. (1992). *A Return to Love*. Harper Collins Publishers. Reprinted by permission of HarperCollins Publishers, Inc.

To Help You Shine

Over the years I've been blessed to be exposed to some incredible people and philosophies. Below are a few of my favorite resources:

Books

Fierce Conversations by Susan Scott
fierceinc.com
425.283.1294

Fish! A Remarkable Way to Boost Morale and Improve Results
by Stephen C. Lundin, Ph.D., Harry Paul, and John Christensen
hyperionbooks.com
800.759.0190

Gung Ho! by Ken Blanchard and Sheldon Bowles
blanchardlearning.com
800.728.6000

See You At the Top by Zig Ziglar
ziglar.com
800.527.0306

Simple Abundance by Sarah Ban Breathnach
simpleabundance.com

The 21 Irrefutable Laws of Leadership by Dr. John C. Maxwell
maximumimpact.com
800.333.6506

Wealth 101: Wealth is Much More Than Money
by Peter McWilliams
Prelude Press
800.LIFE.101 (800.543.3101)

Videos

Celebrate What's Right With the World
starthrower.com
800.242.3220

Fish! Catch the Energy. Release the Potential.
charthouse.com
800.328.3789

Gung Ho!
blanchardlearning.com
800.728.6000

Turn 'Em On, Turn 'Em Loose
tastefullysimple.com/PrinciplesDVD
888.759.2979

Success Coaching

To put the principles of success in your life contact Michael Haynie at missionignition.com or email mike@missionignition.com

Leadership Programs

Pathways to Leadership
pathwaystoleadership.com
800.569.1877